TRUE CRIME
2017

Homicide & True Crime Stories of 2017

Annual True Crime Anthology

By

Jack Rosewood
&
Rebecca Lo

DISCLAIMER:

This anthology of true crime stories from 2017 includes quotes from those closely involved in the cases mentioned, and it is not the author's intention to defame or intentionally hurt anyone involved. The interpretation of the events surrounding the stories are the author's as a result of researching each from a variety of different sources including newspaper stories and interviews, televised interviews and documentaries about the case. Any comments made about the psychopathic, narcissistic or sadistic behavior of the criminals arrested – some among the most prolific serial killers in the country - are the sole opinion and responsibility of the person quoted.

Please notice that this book was released in early December 2017, therefore information about true crime events that occurred in December won't be mentioned in this book.

FREE BONUS!

Get two free books when you sign up to my VIP newsletter at www.jackrosewood.com

150 interesting trivia about serial killers and the story of serial killer Herbert Mullin.

TABLE OF CONTENTS

INTRODUCTION

"I have decided to stick with love.
Hate is too great a burden to bear."

– Martin Luther King, Jr.

Hate is indeed a burden, and as such, it is the dark catalyst for most brutal crimes.

People will say, "Oh, he just went crazy," but inside, there was hatred simmering. Hatred against a loved one who left a heart shattered, the jagged, lovelorn pieces making forgiveness impossible. Hatred against another's country of origin, because the differences create a chasm too vast to attempt to navigate. Hatred against one's own country, inspired by effective propaganda from groups that thrive on hate's dark, festering emotional pull.

In 2017, violence rooted in hate has become almost commonplace.

There's a murder on almost every local news station almost every night–a man shot in his car in one city and another killed in his own home across the county.

Few places are immune.

Mass shootings happen almost every weekend, and for those without a gun, a car, knife or poison seem equally handy.

According to HuffPost, hate crimes rose significantly in 2016, a trend that's continuing in 2017.

While not all of the crimes we've compiled here are hate crimes–we looked at the most scintillating and enticing crimes to lure you in. Most of them are fueled by hate, and that offers an opportunity for a lesson of sorts, a chance to learn from the crimes that occur worldwide so we can thwart them in the future.

"We can't just rail against crime," said Frank Wolf (R-Virginia), an American politician who retired from the House of Representatives in 2015. *"We must speak of the root problems,"* which he said were the breakup of the American family, a culture of violence that has woven its way into our culture and prisoners that are unable to stay out from behind bars due to a lack of programs in place to help them regain their footing in society.

Society, he said, plays a major role in revitalizing our nation and reducing its crime rate.

So, as we hold armchair debates about the reasons behind crime, let's immerse ourselves in some of the year's biggest, most horrifying crime stories, grateful that we ourselves went unscathed, at least for another year.

January

ESTEBAN SANTIAGO-RUIZ
AND 80 SECONDS OF CARNAGE

A stint in the Iraq War serving with the Puerto Rico National Guard left one man with mental health issues severe enough that they ultimately led to murder.

"He lost his mind," said the aunt of 26-year-old Esteban Santiago-Ruiz, a handsome young man with dark hair and dark eyes who used just over a minute–80 seconds total–to wipe five people from the face of the earth.

The shooting rampage occurred on January 6 in the baggage area at Fort Lauderdale-Hollywood International Airport, when Santiago-Ruiz, a Walther 9mm semi-automatic pistol by his side, began shooting after having collected his luggage in the airport's Terminal 2, which housed both Delta Airlines and Air Canada.

According to a news release from the Department of Justice, baggage claim was packed with people who were focused on waiting for the luggage to be transported from the plane to the terminal, leaving room for Santiago to catch them unaware.

"Santiago started shooting, aiming at his victims' heads until he was out of ammunition," the DOJ said in the release.

His victims ranged in age from 57-year-old Michael John Oehme to 84-year-old Olga M. Woltering. One of those killed, 69-year-old

Mary Louis Amzibel, was standing alongside her husband, waiting for the arrival of the plane that would be the last leg of their journey before they were boarding a ship to cruise the Panama Canal. Her husband was also shot, and was perhaps thankfully in a coma in the days following the incident, unaware for a brief time about his wife's death.

One of those at the scene was former White House Press Secretary Ari Fleischer, who tweeted from the airport, "Shots have been fired. Everyone is running."

While the shooting was happening, Fleischer's driver, Mario Andrade of Carey Limousine, was waiting for his passenger near the bottom of the escalator in the Delta baggage area, holding a sign with Fleischer's name on it as he chatted on the phone with another driver. Fleischer, however, had been held up by a late flight, and although he was supposed to arrive at 12:15 p.m., it was nearly 1 p.m.

Already concerned over Fleischer's tardiness, Andrade then heard the accelerated gunfire of what sounded like a semi-automatic weapon, and he dropped to the ground to get out of the line of fire.

As people ran screaming past him, Andrade raised his head from the ground, and saw a man in a blue shirt with a gun in his hand.

In addition to the five people who lost their lives in Terminal 2, six other people were injured in the shooting, while another 36 people were hurt in the panic that followed.

A military background set stage for violence

The New Jersey-born Santiago-Ruiz spent much of his childhood and early adult life in Puerto Rico, where he lived with his mother and brother, until his time with the military led him stateside.

Santiago-Ruiz served three years with the Puerto Rico National Guard, a stint that included almost a year in Iraq.

When he returned home, traumatized after seeing a roadside bomb

4

explode near several of his friends, his behavior became increasingly erratic, and in 2012, Puerto Rican officials temporarily confiscated his firearms, returning them in 2014, just before he joined the Army National Reserves.

When he moved to Alaska in 2014 for work, he joined the Alaska National Guard, although his time with that branch of the military couldn't be classified as a success. After going AWOL several times, he was demoted from specialist to private first class, and eventually the military gave up on him entirely. He was given a general discharge.

There had been warning signs

Santiago-Ruiz's irresponsibility with the military was not the only sign of trouble. The man had a history of domestic violence in his new home in Anchorage, Alaska, where he had moved in 2015 for work. A year before the deadly shooting, he was arrested for attempting to strangle his girlfriend, the mother of his young son, with whom he reportedly had a very volatile relationship.

According to court documents, on the day of this particular assault against her, Santiago-Ruiz was yelling at his girlfriend through the bathroom door before his rage caused him to force his way into the room, "breaking the door, and door frame in the process."

Once inside the bathroom, he turned his rage on his girlfriend, and wrapped his hands around her neck, alternating between strangling her and slapping her on the side of the head, yelling, "get the fuck out, bitch" while he beat her, according to court documents.

The incident was not Santiago-Ruiz's first encounter with Alaska police officials.

A few years prior, Santiago-Ruiz had been investigated for child pornography, and although both weapons and a computer were seized by police, no charges were filed. Things got really frightening when two months before his shooting spree, he walked into the Anchorage FBI office and claimed he was being forced to watch ISIS videos by a U.S. intelligence agency that was controlling his mind.

Based on the mental health implications of the encounter, police were called, and Santiago-Ruiz was sent to a psychiatric hospital.

Unfortunately, according to his brother, Bryan Santiago, his hospital stay was not nearly long enough.

Santiago said his brother was held in an isolated room, under observation for what he believed were the voices that were apparently in his head, influencing his thought process, although doctor-patient privilege kept him from any real details about his brother's hospitalization.

Santiago-Ruiz was held just four days before being released.

"Four days for a guy who talked to the FBI [about] those things ... that is a serious argument, you know? He goes to the FBI saying that he [was] hearing voices, that the CIA are saying that he needs to join ISIS," Bryan Santiago said. "Four days."

Premeditated murder

On Thursday, January 5, Santiago-Ruiz flew on a Delta red-eye flight out of Anchorage, and landed in Minneapolis Friday morning. He then made a connection to Fort Lauderdale.

His flight was anything but peaceful. During one leg of the trip, he got into an argument with a fellow passenger, so by the time he arrived in Fort Lauderdale, his nerves were likely frayed.

Once he'd retrieved his luggage, he went into a bathroom and loaded the Walther 9mm semi-automatic pistol that he'd stowed in his luggage. He began shooting as soon as he exited the men's room.

Five people were killed and six others were injured in the mass shooting. Thirty-six others were hurt in the melee that ensued.

The day after the shooting, federal officials filed criminal charges against him including performing an act of violence at an international airport, using and carrying a firearm during and in relation to a crime of violence, and causing the death of a person through use of a firearm.

He was ordered to be held without bond.

During initial interviews, investigators said Santiago-Ruiz told them he was not only hearing voices, but also believed that the government was controlling his thoughts.

He also confessed that he had been participating in what he called online jihadi chat rooms, which led officials to consider that there were possible terrorist motives for the mass shooting.

"We have not ruled out anything," said George L. Piro, the FBI special agent in charge of the bureau's Miami division, who said that the bureau was considering all motives.

Although no terrorist links were ultimately found in follow-up investigations, Santiago faces the death penalty based on the 22 federal charges formally filed against him.

He has entered a not guilty plea, based on his mental condition at the time of the shooting.

His defense team has said that their client was diagnosed with schizophrenia as well as schizoaffective disorder but was legally competent to stand trial. His lawyers continue to collect evidence to help their client avoid the death penalty.

He initially refused to take his prescribed medication, Haldol, an antipsychotic used in the treatment of schizophrenia, but according to Assistant Federal Public Defender Eric Cohen, he is now strictly adhering to his prescription medication regimen. Still, his mental stability is unlikely to change before he stands trial for the mass shooting, Cohen said.

A judge in March found him legally fit to stand trial, but a trial that was tentatively scheduled for October was expected to be delayed as mental evaluations continued.

All hearings and the trial will be moved to Miami, according to a ruling by U.S. District Court Judge Beth Bloom.

KILLER EXECUTED YEARS
AFTER BRUTAL MURDER SPREE

*"I think you have to be hopeful about life when
you have a child. I think you owe it to them."*

– The late Bryan Harvey

It took 15 years for a Richmond family to finally receive justice, but when justice did come, it was swift.

On January 18, fifteen years after seven people died in a spree killing, one of the perpetrators, Ricky Javon Gray, was executed in Virginia for his role in the crime.

He was pronounced dead at 9:42 p.m. in an execution that was the first to use compounded midazolam, a mix of midazolam and potassium chloride, which led to a request for a stay of execution, which was ultimately denied by the U.S. Supreme Court. A request for death by firing squad was also rejected.

The 2006 murder spree took place over a seven-day period in and around Richmond during the first days of the New Year.

The news first unfolded after a 911 call from the home of the Harvey family, which came after a friend had arrived early for a New Year's Day party only to find the home filling with smoke.

When first responders arrived, they didn't find food burning on the stove, but instead, a fire in the home's smoke-filled basement, along with the bodies of four people, two adults and two children. They had been bound and gagged while the intruders ransacked their home and then killed by using items from their own home, including a kitchen knife and a hammer.

The conditions were so horrific that virtually everyone at the crime scene wept.

The victims were local musician Bryan Harvey, 49, his wife, 39-year-old Kathryn, who owned and operated the toy and novelty shop World of Mirth, and their two daughters, Stella and Ruby, ages 9 and 4.

The 911 call had come from Bryan's bandmate, Johnny Hott, the drummer for their band, House of Freaks, a popular Richmond group.

The murderer–or murderers–had gained entry into the home after Bryan had accidentally left the door ajar after collecting the morning newspaper, making the family an easy target.

The only things that were missing were a laptop, some cash, and Bryan's wedding ring.

The violence was so brutal, so appalling, that it left the city of Richmond in shock and sorrow.

Soon, the outside of the home was awash with flowers, candles, teddy bears, and other mementos signaling a community's grief.

The band Drive-By Truckers released the ballad "Two Daughters and a Beautiful Wife" in 2008 in honor of Bryan Harvey and his family. It tells the story of a confused man who has just died, even though his last memories were of planning to host friends for a celebration.

The band's co-leader, Patterson Hood, wrote the song in honor of the Harveys, who often came to Drive-By Truckers shows, sometimes bringing the girls with them when the concerts were all-ages shows.

He learned of the deaths while watching the news one evening.

"When I saw their pictures my heart nearly stopped," said Hood, who immediately turned to songwriting as therapy to make sense of a senseless, horrific crime. His song uses imagery of heaven to bring comfort not only to himself, but to others who had lost loved ones to violent crimes.

Death penalty brings no relief

As it happened, Ricky Javon Gray and his nephew, Ray Joseph Dandridge, both 28, had been driving around looking for a house to rob when they saw the Harvey family's door ajar.

They had smoked marijuana laced with PCP prior to the murder spree, and it had made them reckless.

Dandridge was sentenced to life in prison, while Gray was sentenced to death.

In 2016, the Supreme Court refused to hear Gray's appeal, and his clemency plea was denied by Governor Terry McAuliffe, who said that Gray's trial was fair, and that the death sentence was an appropriate sentence under Virginia state law.

When asked if he had any last words at his execution at Greenville Correctional Center, his reply was stark, bleak and telling. He only said, "Nope," a much different response than when he made a public apology in a plea for clemency.

Gray based his plea on sexual and physical abuse he suffered as a child.

"I'm sorry they had to be a victim of my despair," Gray said in the audio recording sent to McAuliffe. "Remorse is not a deep enough word for how I feel. I know my words can't bring anything back, but I continuously feel horrible for the circumstances that I put them through. I robbed them from a lifelong supply of joy."

The Harveys were not the only family to die

In the days leading up to the Harvey murders, Gray's wife, 35-year-old Treva Terrell Gray, was found buried in a shallow grave in Washington, Pennsylvania. She had married Gray six months before

11

and lived with the former convict and his nephew in a home owned by her family.

Despite near-constant fighting by the couple, neither Gray nor his nephew were considered suspects in the murder, and Treva's mother, Marna Squires, said that police suggested her daughter had died of a drug overdose.

The night before the brutal Harvey murder, Gray and Dandridge were just getting started.

On that night, they encountered 26-year-old Ryan Carey of Arlington, a city about 100 miles southeast of Richmond, who was attacked so savagely in a robbery that he was in a coma for two weeks and lost the use of his right arm. He later identified the two men who attacked him as Gray and Dandridge, as he vividly described the knife attack during the penalty phase of Gray's trial, causing several jurors to break out in tears.

On January 6, 2006, the police received a call from a Chesterfield resident who was concerned about the well-being of her daughter's friend, 21-year-old Ashley Baskerville, who had been dating Gray at the time, and had lived with both Dandridge and Gray at the Chesterfield home.

When police arrived at the home of Ashley Baskerville's mother, 46-year-old Mary Baskerville Tucker, and stepfather, 55-year-old Percyell Tucker, all three were dead, bound and gagged with tape. While Percyell and Mary had had their throats slit, Ashley had been suffocated with a plastic bag that had been secured with duct tape around her head.

To keep the death penalty off the table for himself, Dandridge pleaded guilty to the Baskerville-Tucker murders and received a life sentence without the possibility of parole.

Killers spill all in confession

On the morning of January 7, 2006, Gray and Dandridge were arrested in Philadelphia, where Dandridge's father, Ronald Wilson, lived and the two had gone in hopes of escaping from the Richmond area undetected.

But at least one of them caved quickly, and about an hour after the arrest, Dandridge confessed to killing the Tuckers and his uncle's girlfriend, Ashley Baskerville.

His partner in crime, however, was a little bit tougher.

It took 12 hours for Gray to break, but when he did, he provided a detailed, three-page confession that included an admission that he beat his wife to death while Dandridge held her down.

In the confessions, both Gray and Dandridge linked Baskerville to the Harvey murders–she was the lookout after the two men entered the house, and she was later found wearing Bryan Harvey's wedding band–as well as to the robbery in her own home.

Originally, Baskerville had intended to pretend to be a victim when her mother and stepfather were robbed to cover up her involvement, but, "things just went wrong," said Dandridge in his confession. In a callous move to prevent Baskerville from growing careless and exposing the two men, Gray decided to kill her, and stole her parents' vehicle as a getaway car.

On February 9, 2006, Gray was charged with five counts of capital murder in the Harvey killings as well as other related murder charges. Dandridge was charged with three counts of capital murder.

While Dandridge initially entered a plea of not guilty, he later amended his plea to avoid the death penalty. He is currently incarcerated at the Keen Mountain Correctional Center in Oakwood, Virginia, living as inmate number 1159354.

AUSTRALIAN MAN KILLED
MANY IN MELBOURNE

January was a difficult month for almost anyone who came into contact with Melbourne man Dimitrious "Jimmy" Gargasoulas, 26, an alleged drug addict whose use of illegal pharmaceuticals only enhanced his mental illness.

Gargasoulas was no stranger to the Melbourne police. Officers in the city knew him well for his illicit drug use, especially heavy use of methamphetamine. According to a friend, mental illness issues believed to be related to schizophrenia and assaults against family members had resulted in numerous police calls to the Gargasoulas residence.

But during the last days of January, the man of Greek-Tongan descent took things farther than he ever had before, and drove his car into a group of pedestrians, killing six people, a third of them children, and injuring 30 more.

His descent into madness had begun earlier in the month, when he began rambling in Facebook posts about "religion, God, Satan, heaven and hell," often not making much sense at all, according to writers who later tried to analyze his posts for clues to his erratic, criminal behavior.

His parents noticed changes in their son, and they essentially wrote him off, which could have led to him turning his car into a weapon of death.

"He's not the Jimmy I used to know," said his father, Chris, who decided to cut the young man out of the family, while his mother, Emily, expressed shame at giving birth to Gargasoulas, and said she hoped her son would "die in hell."

"I don't want to be known that I'm the mother," she said.

14

True days from hell

On the evening of January 18, Gargasoulas started his day by assaulting his neighbor who lived in the same group of apartments, first attacking him with a burning Bible and then punching him, leaving the man disoriented enough that Gargasoulas was able to snatch up his keys and steal his car.

The neighbor, who had previously dated Gargasoulas' mother, Emily, initially tried to deny giving his car keys to the rage-filled young man, but Gargasoulas wasn't taking no for an answer.

It wasn't until Gargasoulas pressed his hand to Wilson's eye and threatened to gouge his eye completely out that Wilson finally complied and turned over the car keys.

"It really hurt, so I said, 'Okay, okay,' and I gave them to him," Wilson said. Car keys in hand, Gargasoulas left, leaving Wilson feeling lucky to be alive.

The next day, Gargasoulas went to a nearby pub, Dog's Bar, where he was refused entrance because the proprietors believed, based on his behavior, that he might have been on drugs.

"He looked like he was on something so we didn't let him in. He was not pleased," said Dog's Bar owner Gavan Green.

Later, in an act of revenge for what he perceived as the previous day's slight, Gargasoulas returned to Dog's Bar and swept the glassware off of two tables on the tavern's terrace, one where women were seated.

The bar's workers tried to stop him and the passenger in his car, believed to be his girlfriend, 25-year-old Akiir Meo, but they were unable to prevent the two from leaving the scene.

According to Green, Meo laughed as the two drove away.

Gargasoulas was busy on Facebook before his attack

Gargasoulas then spewed his wrath on Facebook.

A few days before his attack, Gargasoulas wrote a manifesto against "tyranny" on social media, acting a bit as a self-proclaimed messenger from God as he ominously said the world was "about to change."

That change would come in the form of violence, which started slowly but built up to a blood-soaked rage in the early hours of a Friday morning at his brother's place.

Gargasoulas began his day-long crime spree just before dawn on January 20. His first stop was the flat he shared with his mother and brother, Angelo, 25. There, he stabbed the younger man numerous times, allegedly because he was gay, while Meo, his pregnant girlfriend, screamed in the background and attempted to pull him off his bleeding sibling.

"I tried to pull Jimmy away from Angelo but his face was covered in blood," Meo later said in an interview. "It was the scariest thing I've ever seen."

At the time of the attack, Gargasoulas was due in court on charges of speeding, driving on the wrong side of the road and attempting to elude police.

Instead, after leaving his brother in a pool of blood on the floor of his apartment, he took his girlfriend hostage, telling her that if she didn't come with him, he would have no choice but to kill her and her unborn baby.

She unwillingly accompanied her boyfriend, now virtually a stranger, to the car, where he threatened to kill them both by driving into a light pole while Meo begged him to slow down, to calm down, to stop.

"It shouldn't have happened–I mean, all the people that lost their family and their loved ones, you know, over his stupidity," she said.

But Gargasoulas was determined to see his deadly plans through, and he drove recklessly, doing doughnuts and other dangerous maneuvers with the stolen car along the way.

By now, he was erratic both in his behavior and his thinking, Meo said.

"He kept saying it was the end of the world," said Meo, who was convinced she was going to die that day due to her boyfriend's increasingly erratic behavior, which had now attracted the attention of police, who were following the couple, making the boyfriend even more enraged.

"He just went crazy... He kept saying he was God and he was going to kill lots of people," she said.

After four hours of terror and turbulent driving, Gargasoulas finally stopped to let his terrified girlfriend out of the vehicle on Melbourne's Bolte Bridge over the Yarra River at about 11 a.m., but what was a relief for her and her unborn baby was soon to become a nightmare for others.

Six innocent people die

Alone in the vehicle, he then deliberately drove into a group of more than two dozen pedestrians milling about Melbourne's central business district, using his car as a weapon. He killed six people, including a 10-year-old girl and a three-month-old boy in a stroller, as well as a 33-year-old woman who died later from her injuries. Twenty-six others were injured.

Gargasoulas suffered a gunshot wound to his arm when he attempted to drive away from police, about two minutes after he struck the crowd, and was arrested at the scene.

Meo, who has two children aside from the child she is expecting with Gargasoulas, was horrified that her boyfriend could callously kill a child, especially since he himself has two children from a previous relationship.

A relative of Gargasoulas was not surprised when she heard the news on television.

"Jimmy has always been a bad person," she said, adding that she was devastated to learn that a baby had died in the rage-fueled attack.

Wilson, who owned the car involved in the incident, was also horrified by Gargasoulas' actions behind the wheel of his vehicle, and felt that if he had tried harder to keep the younger man from absconding with his keys, the terrible thing might not have happened at all.

"I feel awful," Wilson aid.

Family expresses support for those suffering

A friend of Gargasoulas said that heavy drug use was responsible for his recent turn toward violence.

The friend blamed crystal methamphetamine (also known as ice), for many of the man's problems, which led to violent outbursts, including the stabbing of his brother and an attack on his mother, as well as a surprise conversion to the Muslim faith.

While the friend made it clear that he was not defending his friend or his friend's actions, he said "that evil drug" ice, which experts say can cause severe mood swings and unpredictable behavior, was responsible for what Gargasoulas did that day in Melbourne.

His father, Chris Gargasoulas, who divorced his sons' mother when both boys were young, took to social media to express sympathy and sorrow for what his son did.

His brother Angelo, despite the violent stabbing incident that left him covered in blood just before the rampage, said "no one could've predicted" what his brother did when he drove his car into a crowd of strangers.

Angelo apparently didn't read his brother's posts on Facebook.

On December 30, he rang in the new year by suggesting to friends that when a police officer was killed in the line of duty, perhaps the "cop killer was the good guy. As it happens, that has been the case more often than not throughout human history. Fuck da police," he wrote.

Angelo, however, was not alone in ignoring those Facebook posts, and he almost paid for it with his life.

A nation responds

Prime Minister of Australia, Malcolm Turnbull, who visited the site with Victorian premier Daniel Andrews and Melbourne lord mayor, Robert Doyle, said, "We are with you in love, and our thanks, our admiration, for the heroism of those who rushed to the aid of the victims."

Numerous tributes were left at the scene as a way to express grief, come together in solidarity and support of the victims and family members and to thank the first responders who helped those who were injured in the incident.

The aftermath

During his first two court appearances, one in April, the other in May, Gargasoulas claimed the Illuminati–a secret society that may or may not be fictitious–made him do it.

He told the court several things in those appearances, including that "the Muslim faith is the correct faith according to the whole world," "I am the savior," "I was under extreme stress, which caused me to have a mental breakdown," "My life is being controlled by the Government," and "I'm very saddened by everything that's happened, but it's due to the Illuminati."

He did not appear at a hearing in August because his lawyers are at work on a plea that Gargasoulas is unfit to stand trial, based on his comments during the first trial.

One of his lawyers, Tass Antos, said his client was too mentally unwell to appear, and a court appearance would not help.

His case is not expected to go to trial until 2019.

February

FAMILY OF FOUR KILLED IN WASHINGTON STATE

A drug deal gone bad could have been the reason behind the brutal deaths of one Washington family, evidence of which the killers attempted to obliterate with fire.

What appears to have been a thriving marijuana business left a Washington family–43-year-old John Careaga, his 37-year-old wife, Christale Careaga, and two 16-year-old boys, his son from a previous relationship, Hunter Schaap, and her son from her first marriage, Johnathon Higgins–dead.

Authorities were alerted to the quadruple homicide, which police said was not a random act, on February 1, when a 911 call came in at about 11:30 p.m., alerting them of violence at a home in Seabeck, Washington, a small seaside town of about 1,000 people.

When Kitsap County Sheriff's deputies arrived, they found the home engulfed in flames. After the fire was out, they found Christale Careaga and the two boys dead in the house.

The home's owner, John Careaga, had last been seen at about 9 p.m., February 2, at Camp Union Store, less than three hours before his family members were found murdered. He purchased a pack of cigarettes.

He was found dead the next day in a neighboring county, his burned body in his torched Ford F-150 pickup truck. A single latex glove was left at the scene.

Murders were not random; family was targeted

Based on the evidence, police detectives did not believe that the murders were random.

"It was a methodical, well-planned event," said Jon VanGesen from the Kitsap County Sheriff's Office, who called on local residents to come forward with any evidence they may have, including conversations, conduct, or any sightings of the vehicle before it had been set ablaze.

While those who killed the blended family tried to cover their tracks by burning both crime scenes, officers still found evidence that could be connected, including 33 marijuana plants and grow lights in the family's garage, as well as $60,000 in cash, some in a safe and more in a dresser. There were also shell casings outside, suggesting that the family was shot to death.

The family owned Christale's Java Hut and Juanito's Taco Shop, a popular mom-and-pop restaurant in town.

Crime Stoppers of Puget Sound is offering a $4,000 reward for any information about the quadruple homicide.

In addition to local police continuing to follow up on leads, detectives have sought the assistance of the FBI, the Bureau of Alcohol, Tobacco & Firearms (ATF) and the Washington State Patrol Crime Lab.

Officials kept mum about many of the details of the crime and the crime scene so as not to compromise the investigation. Police hope that anyone with information in the case will slip up and reveal some bit of information that the media has not yet been given.

In June, police released a video of "a person of interest" in the case, first shown entering a nearby Target store two weeks before the murders, then driving away in a four-door silver sedan.

A GoFundMe page was set up to assist in covering funeral costs as well as costs related to the investigation. As of press time, about $15,000 had been raised.

MAN GOES ON RACIST
TIRADE WITH A GUN

Olathe, Kansas, isn't really a small city. It's the fourth largest city in the state, with a population of just over 150,000 people, but it has a small-town vibe.

So does the sports bar, Austin's Bar and Grill, where just after 7 p.m. on February 22, while bar patrons were watching the University of Kansas basketball team play Texas Christian University, a hate crime erased the city's sense of security.

For Garret Bohnen, a former employee at the bar, the event was frightening because it impacted a place filled with regulars who he saw as family.

On that night in February, the relaxed vibe was shattered by a man who didn't care for some of the other patrons at the bar and didn't mind sharing his opinions out loud.

Racism causes violent outburst

Adam Purinton, 51, was seated at the bar, and believed that two of the men seated near him, Srinivas Kuchibhotla and Alok Madasani, were Iranians. They were, in fact, from East India, and were working for the technology firm Garmin International, a company headquartered in Olathe.

Austin's was just a few miles down the street from Garmin, and the two men often stopped by for a drink after work.

On this night, they encountered a rage-filled Purinton, his face prematurely aged with deep wrinkles.

"Where are you from?" Purinton asked the men. "Why are you here in this country?!"

Madasani went in search of a manager, while Kuchibhotla attempted to diffuse a situation that was not unfamiliar to him as an immigrant.

According to a witness, while Purinton called him a "sand nigger" and said he didn't belong in the United States, Kuchibhotla explained that he and his co-worker from India were in the country legally.

As Purinton continued his angry tirade, several bar patrons began to protest. Purinton was asked to leave, and restaurant staff escorted him from the bar, even as he yelled, "You're going to stick up for them?"

He staggered to his car and left the establishment.

Anger turns to fury

Instead of staying home, however, Purinton went back to Austin's, this time with a gun.

Bar patrons had clustered around the two men in support and were commiserating when another person saw a disgruntled Purinton cross the parking lot, gun in hand.

One of the bar's regulars spotted him and shouted, "He's got a gun," but it was too late.

Purinton burst in through the bar's patio doors and told the two men, "Get out of my country, terrorist," before firing. Kuchibhotla was killed, and Madasani and another man, 24-year-old Ian Grillot, who attempted to chase Purinton after the shooting, were wounded.

"It wasn't right," said Grillot, who was hoping to stop Purinton before he attempted to shoot and kill anyone else.

Tyler Lape, 23, of Olathe, had left the bar about five minutes before the shooting occurred to let his dogs out. He had been hanging out with his friend, Ian Grillot, and said the bar was packed with people watching the University of Kansas basketball team play.

He was incredulous when he heard about the incident on TV and thought what he was seeing was impossible, since he had been there just minutes before.

When he returned to the bar, it had become a crime scene.

Lape wasn't surprised that his friend had intervened on behalf of the two men, and said that he was the kind of guy who would stick up for others in situations like the one that happened at the bar that night.

Executives at Garmin expressed their condolences in a statement and offered grief counselors for employees impacted by the deaths of their co-workers.

What kind of guy was Purinton?

A 1983 graduate of Shawnee Mission North High School, Purinton enlisted in the United States Navy before taking a job at the Wichita airport's air traffic control tower.

He later landed a gig at the Federal Aviation Administration in Olathe, but his love of booze and a failure to report a second DUI to his superiors caused him to be fired.

He later worked as an IT technician at Time Warner Cable, until he failed to show up for work one time too many.

One of his neighbors, Andy Berthelsen, had had a premonition that Purinton was the shooter when he heard it on the news, based on the man's reckless drive down the cul-de-sac where they lived in his black Chevy Silverado, in which he once jumped a curb before almost hitting his garage door when he came to a stop.

According to Berthelsen, Purinton was often drunk, had been arrested for growing marijuana in his basement, and once referred to a black neighbor as "the dark meat" from the safety of the lawn in front of his cream-colored house with pumpkin-orange trim.

He often practiced target shooting outside, until once when Berthelsen complained, which only caused Purinton to move the entire target shooting operation to his basement.

Purinton escapes, but not for long

As a regular in a bar where everyone knew everyone, Adam Purinton was not a fugitive for long.

Soon after the shooting, his neighbors were warned to stay inside while police sent a robot into his garage with a message for him to come out.

Meanwhile, Purinton was checking into a hotel in Clinton, Missouri, almost 100 miles away.

As soon as he was settled, he left his room and headed to the bar at the Applebee's down the street, where he asked the bartender if she and her husband had someplace he could hide because he had "shot and killed two Iranian people" in Olathe.

The bartender immediately called the police. Minutes later, two officers arrested Purinton.

Back at Olathe, a worried wife waits

Meanwhile, Sunayana Dumala was waiting for her husband to come home from work.

She assumed he'd stopped at Austin's for a drink after work, but she was irritated that he was so late, despite the loving note he'd written to her for Valentine's Day the week before: "I can't imagine coming home and not seeing you ... Yours lovingly, Srinu."

When a police car pulled up to the house instead of her husband's Nissan Altima, she fell apart.

But after grieving a few days, she began talking to the press about the state of things in the United States, a melting pot of different cultures that was coming to a full boil as two different sides, one pro-immigration, the other anti, began to clash.

She said that she would continue to push the government to address hate crimes, continuing to seek justice for her husband, who she believed would have done the same.

She also wrote a poignant Facebook post on the plane back to India accompanying her husband's body: "We were planning to expand our own family and had had a doctor's appointment just a few weeks ago. I am writing this as it sinks in that this dream of ours is now shattered."

She said that her husband was an optimist who believed in karma, and often told her that good thoughts and actions would lead to good things returning back to them.

"He used to hug me tightly to sleep, giving me this assurance," she added. "Srinu, now that I have gotten used to that warm hug, I might not be able to sleep."

The aftermath

When Purinton was booked the next day at Henry County Jail, he was charged with first-degree murder and was jailed on a $2 million bond.

In June, he was indicted by a federal grand jury on federal hate crime and gun charges.

According to the indictment, Purinton targeted his victims due to their perceived race, and committed the crimes in a planned and premeditated fashion. He also put others at risk through his actions.

Purinton could face the death penalty if convicted.

"I always had faith that justice would be served," said Kuchibhotla's widow, who met her husband when she was waiting for news on her application for admission to the University of Texas at El Paso, a school she dearly wanted to attend.

She messaged the first person from her hometown whose name came up on the school's admissions list, which happened to be Kuchibhotla's, asking him to check on her application.

After months of chatting, the two fell in love online, and eventually married.

An engineer, Kuchibhotla landed the Garmin job in 2014, and the couple built their dream house on a piece of land in a subdivision surrounded by farmland.

It was looking to be a perfect life until the 2016 election changed the way immigrants were seen in the United States.

Still, while the country's new anti-immigration sentiment was unnerving, Kuchibhotla hadn't been concerned.

Like his friend who died with him at the bar, be believed that goodness would follow them if they kept to themselves and treated others honorably.

Unfortunately, he was wrong. Goodness is sometimes countered by sheer, unadulterated evil.

GIRLS CAPTURE EVIDENCE OF SUSPECTED KILLER

Just before she died, a teenager in Indiana may have made a move to catch her killer.

One of two teen girls killed while spending a day off from school hiking used her cell phone to not only capture video of a man considered the main suspect in the case but also a snippet of his voice, saying, "down the hill."

Family members are calling Liberty German, 14, and Abigail Williams, 13, heroes for having the foresight to take photographs and audio, despite whatever horrors they were experiencing at the hands of a stranger.

They had to be terrified, but despite that, Libby took photos and video, then at some point turned her phone off so the information would go undetected.

"She had the presence of mind to have the phone on and to capture video as well as audio," said Indiana State Police Captain David Bursten.

The girls were hiking at the city of Delphi, Indiana's trail system, part of it repurposed from former railroad tracks. The 10-mile wooded trail has numerous entrance and exit points, and it would normally be busy. But on this February 13, with temperatures never inching above the low 40s, the girls likely had the trail pretty much all to themselves.

So, there they were, uploading photos to Snapchat and enjoying the crisp chill of the winter day, at least until the man in German's video turned up.

The girls never made it back to the spot where they were supposed to be picked up.

They were reported missing by their families at about 5:30 p.m. that day. Hundreds of people, including police, firefighters, friends, family and members of the community searched into the night Monday and into Tuesday morning.

"Having girls of our own, it just hit home," said one of the searchers, Karen Boucher, in an interview with a local newspaper. "We just wanted to do whatever we could."

The teens–Abby, a redhead with freckles and an infectious smile, and Libby, a blond who exuded confidence–were found dead the next day in a heavily wooded area alongside the trail.

Police have not released a cause of death yet, but suspected foul play because of how the bodies were found, on the edge of a creek, against the flow upstream.

They were treating the area like a crime scene because of "the way the bodies were found, that's about all I can say at this time," said Indiana State Police Sergeant Kim Riley, adding that the family expressed their thanks to all the people who participated in the search for the missing girls.

For Carroll County Sheriff Tobe Keazenby, the hunt for the two young girls was taxing both for the community and for police officers.

"It's played tremendously on the emotions of this community," he said.

Girls considered heroes for efforts in solving case, from their watery grave

Liberty German's grandfather, Mike Patty, called both girls "heroes" for being smart enough to surreptitiously capture not only images but also audio of the main suspect in their homicides.

"Both the girls were heroes. They stuck together. I don't know exactly what happened out there that day, but I imagine there was an opportunity for one or both to separate or try in some way to make a break. But those girls loved each other and were good friends. They never left each other's sides. They were both heroes in my book."

That makes the loss of the two girls all the more difficult for the family to bear, Patty added, saying that he instinctively wants to yell to his granddaughter to come down to dinner and to get up for school. The most painful, however, is the time when they would normally arrive home from school, a time that once was boisterous with laughter, and now holds nothing but silence.

The girls had been looking forward to the upcoming softball season, and had already gotten their equipment together and had started practicing, playing catch and working on their batting technique "to hone their skills for the upcoming season. But they'll never get to play a single inning again. There are too many ways to count how our lives will be impacted to share here today," Patty added.

Man in grainy video is suspect because he didn't go to police

While the man captured on Libby German's camera might not be the girls' killer, his unwillingness to turn himself in to police makes him the department's prime suspect.

"He's not just someone we want to talk to; we consider him a suspect in these murders," Sergeant Tony Slocum said. "We're officially calling him a suspect ... our main suspect at this time."

The evidence gathered by the girls, the man photographed on the trail system while the girls were there, along with the fact that the man has not contacted authorities despite two photos of him being released to the media, is only part of what led police to name him as a suspect.

Slocum said the fact that the man hasn't contacted authorities in the days since two photos of him were released is just a tiny part of what led them to describe him as a suspect.

Instead, it is the evidence police have amassed so far that police are targeting the man in the photographs, while speculating how he and the girls might have connected.

While it could have been a chance encounter, the man just happening upon the girls, the more likely scenario, Bursten said, is that someone knew they were going to be there, and went there as well.

DNA evidence is being rushed in order to expedite evidence in the case, which police have been keeping very close to the vest in order to keep the evidence they do have from becoming contaminated with speculation before they get to court.

Too, officials said, revealing too much could make it harder to catch the suspect in a lie.

Many suspects reveal themselves by offering information that the police deliberately withheld from the public during interrogations, and that's what officials are hoping happens in this case.

Memorial honors both girls

Because Delphi is such a small town–only about 3,000 residents call it home–almost everyone turned out for a memorial at Delphi Community High School the day before the Sunday funeral services to pay their respects to the two girls.

A line of mourners wrapped around the school as people waited to enter the building.

Arika Gibson had been friends with Libby since kindergarten, and they still played volleyball and softball together at Delphi Community Middle School.

Because their lockers were side by side, they talked together every day. They also looked a lot alike, and even family members mixed the two up from time to time.

According to Arika, Libby loved being in the school band and loved science, and although she was a whiz at math, and almost always quickly calculated the right answer, she disliked the subject.

Her loves, however, included her family, and she spent as much time with them as she could.

Arika also knew Abby, and said that the girl was fairly quiet in group situations, but when she was with her friends, her personality shined.

"She didn't speak much in front of people, but when she did, her words meant more than words," Arika said.

As for Arika, her friends' murders have led her to consider a career in law enforcement, so that she can use the worst thing to ever happen to her to in her young life to help capture other criminals.

"I'm not gonna let this person take over my life and ruin everything I know and love," she added.

Police hope composite sketch helps

In July, police released a detailed composite sketch of the man seen in the video and by the next day, had received almost 1,000 tips.

The sketch is the first to show the man's face clearly, as in the video, he had his head down, concealing his features.

The sketch is based on a wide range of information the police have received during the course of its investigation.

Abby's mother, Anna Williams, said in an interview with ABC News that the new sketch "means we are just one step closer.

"Nothing you do now is going to bring the girls back. But the person who did this is going to have to pay the consequences for that," she said. "We really truly hope that this is the piece of the puzzle that we need to bring justice to our girls."

The person in the composite is described as a white man with reddish brown hair, between 5 feet, 6 inches, and 5 feet, 10 inches, and weighing between 180 and 220 pounds.

A $230,000 reward is being offered by authorities for information that might solve the murders.

March

SUSPECT IN DECAPITATION
'FELT LIKE' KILLING

18-year-old Oliver Funes Machado clearly hated his mother.

And when police responded to a 911 call to his rural North Carolina home at about 1 p.m. on March 6, they encountered the brutal, gory evidence of that hatred.

Machado was holding his mother's decapitated head in one hand, the butcher knife he had used to severe it from her body in the other.

"When they arrived, he was with the decapitation in his hand and it was a gruesome scene," said Franklin County Sheriff Kent Winstead. "It looked to be a large butcher knife, the weapon that was used. It's a terrible situation for the family, a terrible situation for the neighborhood and this county."

The rest of the woman's body was in the house, between the kitchen and the living room.

According to the Charlotte Observer, as soon as Funes Machado saw the officers arrive at the scene, he placed the head on the ground and was arrested without incident. Charlotte is about 200 miles from Zebulon, where the gruesome murder occurred.

"It was tough, it was a traumatic scene," added Terry Wright of the Franklin County Sheriff's Office, who were summoned to the Zebulon home by Machado himself, who dialed 911 to report the murder.

In the call to the 911 dispatcher, Machado said he stabbed his mother eight times and had left the murder weapon in his mother's mouth.

When he was asked if he had checked on the woman to see if she was still breathing, he told the operator that 35-year-old Yesenia Beatriz Funes Machado was dead.

When asked why he'd killed her, he responded bluntly and said, "Because I felt like it."

Two of his younger siblings, a two-year-old boy and a four-year-old girl, were inside the home at the time of the murder, and likely heard their mother's screams as their brother savagely took her life, finishing the bloody murder by sawing off the head of the woman who gave birth to him. His father, however, was not at home, and a 14-year-old brother was at school. The younger children were unhurt physically, but mentally, they will likely have scars that will never fully heal.

Neighbor paints a horrifyingly vivid portrait

"I can't imagine how anyone could do that to anybody, much less your own mother," said neighbor Randy Mullins, 59, who was leaving his house just as the deputy arrived at the scene, and spotted first the head, about five feet in front of the porch in the front yard, then the deputy's horrified face.

Mullins said he could see the revulsion the deputy was experiencing wash across his face at the scene. He stopped to ask the deputy if he needed any help, but the deputy, who was cuffing Machado's hands behind his back, said no.

Mullins returned home and told his 91-year-old mother to stay inside as six more law enforcement vehicles arrived at the scene.

"I couldn't believe it. Things like that don't happen," added

Mullens, who had lived in the neighborhood for 25 years. "You can't believe somebody would do that. You hear about that, but it never happens across the street from you."

Worse, he said, was the degree of calm the suspect exhibited as he sat handcuffed as the deputy attempted to comfort the horrified younger children who had seen the crime unfold.

"He was sitting there like he didn't have a care in the world," Mullins said, adding that the killer wasn't showing any signs of remorse, he wasn't crying, and he wasn't upset by what had just occurred.

Another neighbor, Leona Smith, told reporters that she had seen the two children outside, sobbing over losing their mother in such a violent manner.

She, too, was surprised that such a horrific crime could happen in a quiet neighborhood to a seemingly normal family living in a traditional house with a white picket fence, a trampoline and a swing set in the backyard.

"It was heartbreaking," she said.

Worse still was when the husband came home, and the sounds of his anguished cries could be heard throughout the usually serene neighborhood.

Machado was in the country illegally from Honduras, according to U.S. Immigration and Customs Enforcement, but is believed to qualify for DACA (Deferred Action for Childhood Arrivals) status.

Counselors were called in to help the 20 first responders who were at the scene emotionally cope with what they saw.

Mental problems led to murder

According to the teen's public defender, C. Boyd Sturges III, psychiatric issues likely played a role in the murder.

"This is something that's going to take weeks and months for us to get some answers as to why this happened," said Franklin County District Attorney Michael D. Waters said it could take months to determine exactly why Machado killed his mother in such a heinous fashion.

Machado was initially charged with first-degree murder in his mother's death and was held without bond.

In November, however, murder charges against him were dropped because he was found not mentally fit to stand trial because mental health professionals determined he was not able to understand the charges against him or participate in how his own defense at trial.

Maternal decapitations aren't so rare

In 2015, in Florida, Christian Gomez cut off the head of his mother, 48-year-old Maria Suarez Cassagne, and stashed it in a garbage can. The 23-year-old blamed it on his mother's "nagging."

Edmund Kemper, the so-called "Co-ed Killer," beheaded his mother on Good Friday in 1973 after beating her to death with a claw hammer. After using the severed head for oral sex, he nailed it to the wall so he could use it as a macabre dart board. He then cut out her vocal cords and sent them down the garbage disposal. "That seemed appropriate, as much as she'd bitched and screamed and yelled at me over so many years," he said after his arrest.

April

TWO-MONTH MARRIAGE ENDS IN MURDER-SUICIDE AT ELEMENTARY SCHOOL

San Bernardino has had its share of high-profile crimes.

In 2015, a couple shot and killed 14 people at an office holiday party in a terrorist attack.

And on April 10 of this year, a domestic violence situation turned into a school shooting that left one couple and a special needs student dead.

Short-lived wedding ends in murder-suicide

Cedric Anderson had been married to Karen Elaine Smith just over two months when he walked into her classroom at North Park Elementary School, something that wasn't abnormal at the school, which often saw spouses visiting during the school day. (He had originally attempted to enter through a locked side door, according to closed-circuit camera footage that was later reviewed.)

On this day, however, instead of delivering lunch or a bouquet of flowers or some other treat for his new bride (he had told staffers he had something to drop off for her), he pulled out a .357 magnum revolver and shot the woman he had professed to love forever just 60 or so days ago, fatally wounding her as well as a child standing behind her.

40

He fired 10 shots without saying a word, at some point stopping to reload his weapon, injuring another student in the classroom, then turned the gun on himself, fatally shooting himself, police said.

According to San Bernardino Police Chief Jarrod Burguan, the couple, both 53 years old, had been together for about four years before finally tying the knot in late January. Apparently, shortly after that ceremony, the two separated, although according to those closest to the couple, Anderson was trying to win back his bride. Smith, however, was reluctant to return to the home she'd briefly shared with her husband.

"Those closest to her said that she had mentioned that his behavior was odd and that she was concerned about his behavior, and that he had made some threats toward her," Burguan said in a news conference.

Burguan said that Anderson did not specifically threaten to shoot her, and his wife did not take the threats he made seriously.

She had also not shared her troubles with her co-workers at the elementary school where she was a special-education teacher, and kept her private life to herself, Burguan added.

Facebook shows a happy relationship

Right after the wedding, Anderson posted a video of himself and his wife on their honeymoon titled, "I married a crazy hiker! I got to get in shape."

There were sweet moments between the two, with no signs of what was to come.

"Say how much fun you're having, baby," he told Smith in the video, his arm draped around her shoulders.

"Hi," she said, smiling. "We're having such a good time."

"She got me hiking," Anderson added. "We're having a ball. It's been nice."

According to Joshua Smith, Smith's son from a previous relationship, his mother was a "genuinely loving and caring person," devoted to her Christian faith.

And at first, it seemed like Anderson, a pastor, was the perfect man for her.

Anderson, they soon found out, was "paranoid and possessive," which prompted Smith to leave him just months after the wedding.

It was a decision that would ultimately lead to her death, and leave her son shocked that his mother will not get the chance to see her granddaughter grow up, and that he will never hear his mother's voice again except in his memory.

Problems began almost immediately after wedding vows

According to Smith's mother, as soon as Smith and Anderson were married, her perfect pastor turned into someone else entirely.

"She thought she had a wonderful husband, but she found out he was not wonderful at all," said Irma Sykes, 80. "He was a wolf in sheep's clothing. As soon as they married, he turned on her."

Shortly after the wedding, Anderson started accusing his new wife of cheating, and began threatening to throw her out the window if he learned his suspicions were true.

Smith, however, was a strong woman and was not interested in a paranoid, abusive spouse at this particular point in her life, so she left her new husband, the ink barely dried on their wedding license.

She'd obtained her teaching credentials late in life after her children were grown, in order to help others, and she didn't want anything to mar her mid-life happiness.

Her new husband fluctuated between angry and cajoling after she left him, sometimes enraged that she had been so bold, other times attempting to win her back by saying what he believed to be all the right things.

Smith, however, was not going to fall for any sweet nothings coming from the mouth of a man whom she'd realized was nothing but poison. And that, her mother said, was the reason why she died.

A little research into her new husband's past might have saved Smith's life.

As it turns out, Smith was not the first woman Cedric Anderson had abused.

In 1996, after their 11-year marriage came to an end, Anderson threatened Natalie Anderson, the mother of his three children, to the point she needed to take out a restraining order to protect herself.

After she refused to pay for their divorce, Anderson threatened to kill Natalie, their children and himself. A few months later, he told her that he would pick up the children from school and she would never see them again.

In June of 1997, she again saw Anderson's rage when he dropped their three sons off at her house after visitation, which led to another request for a restraining order.

"He refused to leave and ended up jumping on me and choking me. He did this in front of his sister," she said.

She called the police, who wanted to arrest Cedric Anderson, but Natalie didn't want her children to see their father in handcuffs, so she dropped the charges.

It could have been a deadly mistake.

"Since then, the respondent has been threatening to kill me," Natalie Anderson said, not only to her, but to others in the ministry, Natalie's mother, Anderson's sister and friends the couple shared.

Another former partner, live-in girlfriend 50-year-old Jennifer Lindsey, also sought a restraining order after the Christian minister nearly killed her in 2013 over plans she'd made to sing karaoke with a female friend.

In the middle of the night on May 17, 2013, "He suddenly pulled the blankets off of me and then grabbed me by my arms. He then put the pillow over my face and held it so I could not breathe," Lindsey wrote in her paperwork for the restraining order.

"I fought as hard as I could, kicking with my feet. He still had one of my wrists and continued to push the pillow down into my face. I thought I would die that night," said Lindsey, who finally managed to break free.

Still, she didn't leave, and a week later, Anderson attacked her while she was ironing clothes for a Memorial Day dinner the two were planning.

"Cedric shoved me with his hand to my throat, pushing me onto the bed," she said. "He had a butcher knife in his hand and told me he was sick of me."

Luckily, she escaped with her life.

Students loved student who died in domestic shooting

Jonathan Martinez, a student who was seated behind Karen Smith when she was shot and was also fatally wounded, was born with Williams syndrome, a genetic condition that is accompanied by developmental delays, learning disabilities, and cardiovascular disease. Williams syndrome impacts 20,000 to 30,000 people in the United States, and according to a website about the condition, "children with Williams syndrome tend to be social, friendly and endearing."

That was true of Jonathan Martinez.

Kerrie Oestreich, a recreational aide at the school, said that because she greeted children as they got off the bus each day, she was the first adult person Jonathan saw each day.

"He was always happy, even if he was sick," Oestreich said.

"Sometimes he'd get off the bus and tell me, 'Miss O, I think today my foot's going to hurt,'" she added with a chuckle. "I'd be like, 'Okay, Jonathan, I'll check on you later.' And he'd just bounce right on up with the rest of the kids."

Another student, Nolan Brandy, 9, was also behind Smith and was hit in the upper body, but he is expected to survive.

Grief is overwhelming for many

Initially, Oestreich said she thought a grounds crew was doing maintenance when she heard the first shot.

When Anderson fired the second shot, that's when she and the other faculty members within earshot realized that they were hearing gunshots.

She went into the hall where she ran into some children that she safely hid in the bathroom then she herself was led to a classroom on lockdown.

The pain of losing her coworker is overwhelming, Oestreich said, comparing the physical anguish to the loss of her father.

For the students, the images will live with them for a very long time.

Brianna Alcazar was in Smith's classroom when the shooting occurred.

"I heard him load a gun," Brianna said, speaking softly to a reporter. "And then I saw his gun was black and his jacket was black."

She said Anderson said nothing before he started shooting, and that she loved her teacher, Karen Smith, who taught her how to read.

"I miss her—I want her to come back," she said.

Other children heard the shooting

According to parents and other witnesses, the walls between classrooms were not thick enough to keep the sounds of bullets and terror from being heard by young students outside the classroom.

Jane Muschell told the Washington Post that her 9-year-old son, Jeremy, who knew Jonathan and exchanged greetings with him every day, was returning from a bathroom break when he heard four gunshots.

"They were really, really loud, and he heard people yelling, 'No, don't!'" Muschell said. "He told me he heard [Anderson] reload the gun—cocking the gun."

Jeremy's teacher led the students out an emergency door to the playground to wait for police in a safer place.

Muschell said the entire event happened so fast that her 9-year-old son didn't even have a chance to cry, even though he was terrified. Instead, teachers helped the children focus on getting out of the classroom and finding somewhere safer to wait for help.

Classroom was chaotic during shooting

When Anderson entered the room where Smith taught, there were 15 students and two aides in the special-needs classroom, which included students in first grade through fourth grade.

According to survivors, Anderson said nothing, but students or aides yelled, "No, don't," when Anderson pulled out his weapon and took aim at his new bride.

Police, parents question school safety

According to the San Bernardino school district, policies at all the district's schools changed after the 2015 terror attack.

"Once the school bell rings, the only entry point into a campus is the main school office, where visitors have to sign in and receive a visitor's pass," according to district spokeswoman Maria Garcia.

According to Burguan, Anderson gained entrance by telling

administrators he had something to drop off for his wife, which was not an uncommon way for spouses of faculty and staff to gain access to the school campus.

Those policies, which a year ago seemed strict, have now been tightened even more in the wake of the shooting.

Because of the incident, fingerprinted volunteers will now be the only non-staff members allowed through the campus office into the classrooms at North Park Elementary School, according to school district Superintendent Dale Marsden.

"After I spoke to Virginia Tech, Columbine, and Sandy Hook, they all had some of the same advice," Marsden said. "It's not a marathon, it's a sprint. We have a lot of emotion now, but we want to make the decision after careful consideration."

Meanwhile, the community united in prayer and tears.

"Sometimes all we can do is cry. And today is the day for that," said Bishop Gerald Barnes of the Diocese of San Bernardino. "We'll get up again, we'll move on, we'll become stronger. But today is the day to cry, that we have come to such a state."

May

IT WAS NOT A GOOD MOTHER'S DAY FOR ONE OREGON MOM

Fifty-nine-year-old Tina Webb of Colton, Oregon, had been married for almost 40 years, and had raised a family she believed loved her as much as she loved them.

Their 36-year-old son, Joshua Lee Webb, lived in a renovated barn on the family's property because he had difficulty with his eyesight and needed his parents to look after him. His constant companion was a dog he'd asked his parents to get for him, and as far as Tina was concerned, country life in Oregon was bliss.

Evidently, however, she was wrong.

And on Mother's Day, which fell on May 14 this year, she found out how horrifyingly wrong she was when Joshua stabbed his mother to death, wielding his butcher knife so hard that he ultimately decapitated her. Leaving behind no witnesses, he also killed his beloved dog.

Drenched in his mother's blood, Joshua then drove his mother's 2011 Chevrolet Equinox to the nearby Harvest Market in Estacada, about 12 miles away. His mother's decapitated head was on the seat next to him.

When he arrived at the store at about 2:15 p.m., he grabbed his mother's head and ran into the store, trailing blood. His first words were, "You better run," to the first clerk he saw, but the stunned clerk didn't get very far. Joshua Webb then stabbed the man with his bloodied knife seven times.

Still, despite his injuries, the clerk, along with other store workers, was able to detain Webb, wrestling him to the floor and taping his hands and feet to immobilize him, while horrified shoppers ran to the diner next door to call 911.

"It was traumatic, but it happened so fast that nobody really saw what was going on," said Marvin Flora, the diner's owner, adding that one hysterical woman did say that she saw someone carrying the bloody head in his arms.

After he was captured, all the emotions that led to his multiple attacks left him, and he was deflated, witnesses said, a nearly blind man lying on his stomach on the grocery store floor, now slippery with blood.

"He didn't say anything after he was subdued," said interim Sandy Police Chief Ernie Roberts, who responded to the 911 call. "He was in like a catatonic state, wasn't speaking to anybody."

The only thing he said to those around him was that he was thirsty.

A family left shell-shocked

Tina Webb's headless body was discovered by one of her daughters, Sarah Morris-White, an unwelcome surprise during a Mother's Day visit.

She told police she'd arrived at the home about 45 minutes after neighbors saw her brother drive away in her mother's vehicle and found her mother's body near the front door.

Horrified, she went to a neighbor's house and asked them to call 911.

She told them as they waited for police that she had also found her brother's new dog, dead on the kitchen counter.

A neighbor called the incident "a nightmare," something that was completely unimaginable in the bucolic community that they all called home.

Tina Webb's husband was left devastated, and fumbled for the right words to express his anguish in interviews with the press.

"My wife was wonderful," Tina's husband, David Webb, said in an interview. "I've been married to her for almost 41 years. Joshua was our son. I never saw a problem. Evidently there was one. I don't know. I start crying every time I think about it.

"I never foresaw a problem. If I had I would have stopped it," he added through sobs. "I just can't believe I lost my wife and my son in one day. ... I don't know. I wish I did. I wish I had some answers, but I don't. I waited all my life to retire with my wife, and now I can't. That's all I know."

Wounded clerk survived attack

Mike Wagner, the 66-year-old man who was stabbed by Webb, was airlifted to a Portland hospital, Legacy Emanuel Medical Center, about 25 miles from the store, which soon was covered with homemade get well soon signs as well as balloons.

His wife, Pamela Wagner, wrote about the incident on Facebook, calling her husband "a tough cookie" who will recover from the tragedy that occurred at his place of employment.

"This is such a crazy random thing that has happened, and I am truly at a loss why someone would do what this person did," she wrote, advising those reading her post to hug their loved ones "a little tighter" that night.

Wagner loved telling jokes and leaving his customers feeling better than they had before they entered the small-town store.

He was also an honest worker, no hint of used car salesman in his sales pitch, and would tell customers which fruits and vegetables were ripe and worth buying, and which would be a tasteless, mealy waste of money.

Connie Tumaniszwill, 71, had been at the store that Mother's Day but had left about an hour before Webb arrived.

"Everyone is family here, and we all take care of each other," she said. "When something like this happens, we all feel it. We're just so thankful that he survived. If we lost him, this town wouldn't be the same."

Friends surprised by Webb's actions

According to his Facebook page, Webb was in a relationship, but neighbors said that his partner had recently moved out of Oregon.

For Webb, whose eyesight issues made many things difficult, her move could have been seen as a devastating blow that negatively impacted his entire life.

Still, friends were astonished over what happened.

One such friend, 34-year-old Curtis Strandy, said that Webb loved his mother, and had never been violent on any occasion, which made the gruesome murder so much harder for him to believe.

"Everything good about humanity, he had in him," Strandy said, adding that Webb was "the nicest guy" he's ever met.

Still, based on the criminal annals of history, it's almost always the nicest guys who seem to commit the most savage of crimes.

Prior to the murder of his mother, Webb had only had one charge against him - the unlawful use of metal objects on tires-a 2000 charge for which he was convicted.

During his first court appearance on May 17, Webb was charged with murder, attempted murder, first-degree abuse of a corpse, and first-degree animal abuse. He was ordered to be held without bond.

Tina Webb was a master gardener who donated flowers to local churches to beautify their grounds.

A neighbor, Rhonda Durham, was grateful that the woman's hobby had provided her things of beauty to remember her by, as she has perennials including irises and hostas that were given to her by Webb that will bloom every year.

Those plants are things "that I'm going to treasure now forever," Durham said.

Ex-girlfriend may offer clues

According to the girlfriend who moved out of Oregon at the behest of her boyfriend, Heather Suydam, Webb began acting strangely about two months before the Mother's Day murder.

A Clackamas County homicide detective who interviewed Suydam said that Webb began rubbing the left side of his head almost obsessively, then suddenly turned deeply religious, breaking things off with the woman he professed to love on Facebook, telling her he never wanted to see her again.

Suydam moved back to her home state of Massachusetts, where Webb surprisingly called her in early April, about a week after the split, to tell her about what he described as an "odd pulsing sensation" he was having in the back of his head.

Still, in the days before the murder, Webb was considering a reconciliation with his girlfriend and had talked with his father about traveling to Massachusetts to see her.

"He said his son was in good spirits," according to police.

On the day Nancy died, David Webb left for work at 5 a.m. for his 30-mile commute, and called his wife at around 8:30 a.m. to wish her a happy Mother's Day and ask her if she wanted to go out to dinner that night.

It was, he said, the last time he spoke to his wife.

WHEN TWO TERROR GROUPS COLLIDE, OUTCOME CAN BE DEADLY

It would be rare for Timothy McVeigh to be seen as a hero.

But for one small neo-Nazi group, McVeigh had made a big move that had attracted the attention of a nation, and some members had a morbid fascination with the man because of it.

McVeigh was an American domestic terrorist who was convicted of detonating a truck bomb in front of the Alfred P. Murrah Federal Building in Oklahoma City in 1995, killing 168 people, many of them children at a day care center on the second floor of the building, and injuring more than 600.

His picture was framed on a dresser in one of the bedrooms in the Tampa, Florida, apartment where two roommates died and two went to prison after neo-Nazi ideals somehow went horribly wrong.

The four young roommates were members of the neo-Nazi group Atomwaffen (German for atomic weapon) Division, a group founded in Florida that recruits at universities nationwide.

One was a member of the Florida National Guard, two worked temporary jobs at a local recycling plant and talked about joining the military, if only to bone up on their target practice, and the fourth spent his days playing video games.

Their apartment included guns, ammunition, and bomb-making materials, enough for them to make bombs to rival those of Timothy McVeigh, if that was what they were after. And it seemed that that might have been their ultimate goal.

At least it was, until one of the men, easily swayed by the opinions of others, converted to Islam instead.

On May 19, the Army National Guard member, Brandon Russell,

54

22, returned home from a training session to find two of his roommates, Jeremy Himmelman, 22, and Andrew Oneschuk, 18, the two recycling plant workers still trying to determine their futures, dead of gunshot wounds to the head in the Tampa townhouse they shared with 18-year-old Devon Arthurs.

Russell was outside of the apartment, still wearing Army camouflage and reeling from the horrible find inside when Arthurs turned up with police, telling them that his distraught roommate had no idea what had transpired in the apartment while he'd been away.

Were video games code for Islam conversion?

So, what was going on?

Arthurs had just been arrested at the nearby Green Planet Smoke Shop, where he went with the semiautomatic pistol, a weapon different from the one he'd used to kill his roommates, and took several people there hostage.

It was at 5:30 p.m. that May evening when a bloodied Arthurs went to the shop, where he encountered one employee and a customer, and went on a verbal rampage.

According to the smoke shop manager, Fadi Soufan, who was speaking on behalf of the shaken employee that was at the store when the incident happened, Arthurs came into the smoke shop and told both the employee and her customer to get on the floor.

"Do me a favor and get the fuck on the ground!" he yelled to a female employee and male customer, before asking the customer, "Why shouldn't I kill you?"

A few minutes later, when another customer entered the store, he, too, was ordered by Arthurs to get on the ground.

He then told them that he had already killed someone and bragged about "blasting their heads."

He then began to rant about the state of society, which had led him first to neo-Nazism, then to Islamic extremism.

"He told them the world was corrupt," said Soufan, adding that the visit to the smoke shop was mostly to draw attention to what he saw as his cause.

"He wanted publicity. Actually, he pointed at the camera," Soufan said. "He said he wanted CNN to come."

Arthurs spent just five minutes inside the store ranting, but it was enough time to sweep items off a shelf, demand a Coke from the store cooler, and scare the living daylights out of three innocent people.

According to a report filed by Tampa Police Detective Kenneth Nightlinger, he told his three hostages that he was angry over the United States bombings in "his" Muslim countries.

And although CNN didn't show up, the police thankfully did, and after one hostage ran out of the store, officers were able to persuade Arthurs to let the other two leave as well.

After a few minutes of negotiating, officers were able to arrest Arthurs before he could injure anyone else.

When he was arrested, he introduced himself as Khalid, and told police that he was sympathetic to ISIS causes.

After seeing blood on Arthurs, police asked if anyone else was hurt, and he said, "The people in the apartment, but they aren't hurt, they're dead. I had to do it.

"This wouldn't have had to happen if your country didn't bomb my country," added the Florida-born teen.

How does a neo-Nazi find radical Islam?

On the surface, both neo-Nazis and radicalized Islamic terrorists are not so far apart.

Both groups believe that their people are superior to others and both also believe that they are right to work toward the extinction of those who oppose their desire to force the rest of the world to conform to their beliefs.

But how does one go from one extremist group to another?

According to former white nationalist Watson Fincher, people who feel as though they are on the fringes of society are easily swayed by almost any belief.

Fincher said Arthurs "would jump from one ideology to the next... He was an atheist. Then Catholic. Then Orthodox Christian. Then Nazi. Then Muslim. He latched onto the esthetics of anything that looked cool."

At any rate, by most accounts, on the day of the murder, he was Islam, and his neo-Nazi roommates had to die.

Arthurs initially told police that'd he'd killed his roommates because he'd converted to Islam, and they'd offended him by making light of his new religion. (He made references to "Allah Mohammed" as officers led him to the patrol car after he surrendered at the smoke shop to secure his case.)

According to police, Arthurs told them his roommates had "disrespected his Muslim faith," which he viewed as part of a growing global anti-Muslim sentiment that wasn't acceptable in his eyes.

Later, however, after he was charged with murder in the deaths of his two roommates, he said he was preventing a terrorist attack being planned by his former neo-Nazi group Atomwaffen, which experts estimate has only a few dozen members nationwide.

"I prevented the deaths of a lot of people," Arthurs said in a statement, adding that the group intended "to build a Fourth Reich" to succeed efforts begun by the Holocaust of Nazi Germany.

When they got to the apartment building, Russell was standing just outside the door, police said, clearly upset over the murders of his roommates.

Arthurs was quick to tell police that Russell had not been part of Arthurs' plan to kill his roommates, which he'd done while Russell was away.

Inside, Himmelman and Oneschuk were dead of gunshot wounds to the head and chest.

As it happens, neo-Nazis and Islamic extremists can't be friends

While it would seem as the two extremist groups with similar missions would be capable of uniting, even the white supremacist publication the Daily Stormer scoffed at Arthurs and his conversion to Islam.

"Atomwaffen are a bunch of good dudes. They've posted tons of fliers with absolutely killer graphics at tons of universities over the years," a writer at the publication said in a post. The group, however, made one mistake, and that was trusting a convert to Islam.

According to the Daily Stormer editor, Andrew Anglin, Arthurs had been making online attempts at converting readers to Islam, a move that had led Anglin to ban him from their server.

Anglin also said that Arthurs had likely tarnished the reputation of Atomwaffen Division, at least as far as other neo-Nazi groups were concerned.

"Atomwaffen Division, are considered a potential threat because they're aligned with Islamic terrorists and are encouraging attacks on the United States," Anglin wrote.

Before he had a chance to mourn, Russell was also in handcuffs

Despite his grief, Russell was arrested about a week later during a traffic stop after police found a garage stocked with bomb-making materials during their initial search of the murder scene. Items including a cooler full of hexamethylene triperoxide diamine (HMTD), a cake-like explosive, as well as chemicals that can be mixed to make explosives, including potassium chlorate, potassium nitrate, nitromethane and a package of ammonium nitrate addressed to Russell, the same chemical used by McVeigh in the Oklahoma City bombing. There were also other bombmaking materials, along with Nazi and white supremacist propaganda.

Russell attempted to suggest that the bomb-making materials were used for homemade rockets and other projects he'd undertaken while a student at the University of South Florida, but even the FBI didn't buy that excuse.

According to FBI Special Agent Timothy A. Swanson, HMTD is "too volatile" for those types of projects, adding that the amount found in the garage would "constitute a 'bomb' under federal law."

Russell's alibi was further thwarted by Arthurs, who threw his former roommate under the bus by telling authorities that he knew Russell had participated in "online neo-Nazi internet chat rooms where he threatened to kill people and bomb infrastructure," likely something Arthurs, a scrawny, pigeon-faced young man, likely also did before he found a new religion.

He also told authorities that Russell "loved Timothy McVeigh," and believed the only mistake McVeigh made was using too little material, so the entire building didn't collapse after the truck bomb was detonated.

Russell was the leader of the Atomwaffen and posted as "Odem" online.

In one post he wrote: "The Atomwaffen Division is a group comprised of many members and has been many years in the making, at least three years. Our exact numbers are not to be talked about too publicly but we are over 40 members strong. Large concentration in Florida, various smaller chapters throughout the

US, such as Chicago, Texas, and New England, Boston, New York, Kentucky, Alabama, Ohio, Missouri, Oregon, Virginia, and a few others."

The Atomwaffen Division is considered a hate group by both the Anti-Defamation League and the Southern Poverty Law Center. It targets universities with propaganda fliers, including the University of Boston, the University of Central Florida, and State College of Florida Manatee-Sarasota.

Still, Russell was not arrested that day, even though behind bars seems an ideal place for the white supremacist with the bomb-making materials to be, especially during a time when racially-charged incidents seem to be escalating.

What about the victims?

In the aftermath of the murders, the families of both Jeremy Himmelman and Andrew Oneschuk did their best to segregate their sons from the neo-Nazi group their killer said they were associated with.

The families of both young men said they were interested in joining the military and were not involved in the white supremacist group that Arthurs and Russell headed.

Lyssa Himmelman said Arthurs was lying when he said that all four roommates were neo-Nazis, and said that both men had planned to move out of the apartment due to the other duo's extreme views.

She called Jeremy Himmelman a "sweet, funny, amazing loving brother who would never hurt a fly. He was a wonderful guy."

However, Himmelman's girlfriend, Kianna Kaizer, said that although his far-right beliefs did not dominate his life, they were absolutely a part of it.

"Jeremy went through a lot of struggle in his life, and national socialism offered him the rigidity he desired, and offered him

60

solutions for the things out of his control," Kaizer said. "So, it's been really hard to try and tell his family, but yes, he did hold white supremacist beliefs."

Oneschuk's Facebook page features photos supporting President Donald Trump, but friends said they were unaware of any white supremacist beliefs.

Still, members of Atomwaffen called Oneschuk and Himmelman fallen heroes or Aryan brothers, even as they castigated Arthurs as a race traitor.

Andrew Oneschuk's father, Walter, said that their son's alt-right views began in high school, when the conservative young man's values took such a detour that Walter was forced to block his son from access to racist and anti-Semitic content.

"He looked at his generation and said, 'We're on the path to ruin,'" Walter said.

However, Walter believed that a trip to France along with a short stint in the French Foreign Legion may have helped tame his extremist views.

"He was a different kid when he came back," he said. "He realized this stuff was not his future."

According to Kaizer, however, both were Atomwaffen members, although Oneschuk and Himmelman were part of the group's Massachusetts branch until moving to Florida to be part of the faction Russell headed.

Members question group's portrayal

Despite the bomb-making supplies and violent YouTube videos that serve as recruitment materials for Atomwaffen, members don't consider themselves a hate group.

"I'm a neo-Nazi. I'm not a monster," said 20-year-old William

Tschantre, who was with Russell when he was arrested. "We're not here to, like, bomb the U.S. government. That's absolutely ridiculous."

According to Tschantre, both Oneschuk and Himmelman were irritated by Arthurs' attempts to encourage them to convert to Islam, and on the night before the shooting, Arthurs was arguing online with other members of Atomwaffen over his own conversion.

"I told them to calm down," Tschantre said.

Although the two victims were not involved, the exchange did grow heated, which could have carried over into the apartment's already tense atmosphere.

The morning after the shooting, Russell drove to Tschantre's home in nearby Bradenton, about 46 miles south of Tampa, and told him what had happened.

"I could tell by the look on his face he wasn't joking," Tschantre said. "He was on the verge of tears."

To support his group leader, Tschantre quit his job as a fast-food restaurant and grabbed $3,000 in cash as they debated where to hide out.

They at first considered turning to Russell's father, a sheriff's deputy in West Palm Beach, but instead chose to flee to the Florida Keys.

The two bought rifles and ammo at a sporting goods store, Bass Pro Shops, a move that suggests they were planning for future violent confrontations, then spent the night in a Miami hotel.

Thankfully, however, Russell was arrested the next morning at a Burger King in Key Largo without incident.

FBI agents have filed explosives charges against Russell, who could face 11 years in prison.

Aftermath

A week after his arrest, Arthurs asked to talk to police.

Officers spent about ten minutes in his cell discussing his case.

"He spent much of the ten minutes talking about how he believed his family's safety was in jeopardy," wrote the deputy who responded to Arthurs' request, mostly because Atomwaffen members would be likely to seek revenge for the killings of their members, and Arthurs' family members would be good targets.

He also said someone had broken into his social media account to post obscene pictures and that one of his roommates took pleasure in bragging "about how many Muslims his father has killed as a Navy SEAL."

Arthurs faces two counts of first-degree murder, two counts of aggravated assault, and three counts of armed kidnapping.

Prosecutors have said that they do not intend to seek the death penalty in Arthurs' case.

Instead, he faces the possibility of life in prison without a chance for parole.

"One way or another, we don't really care whether he gets the death penalty or not, as long as he spends the rest of his life in prison and a very uncomfortable life in prison," said one victim's father, Walter Oneschuk.

Manchester bombing kills 22 at Ariana Grande concert

"Broken. From the bottom of my heart, I am so, so sorry. "Don't have words," wrote Ariana Grande on Twitter following a bombing at her May 22 concert that left 23 people dead and more than 500 injured.

The Islamic terror attack occurred when a homemade bomb detonated just as people were leaving the Manchester Arena following Grande's concert.

The bomber, Salman Ramadan Abedi, acted alone, police said, but police said others were aware of his plans.

The Arena foyer turned deadly

About 21,000 people had attended Grande's 2017 Dangerous Woman Tour concert and were excitedly making their way out of the arena, eager to meet up with parents or friends in the foyer, when the improvised explosive device the 22-year-old Britain-born Abedi had fashioned, packing it with nuts and bolts to act as shrapnel, went off at about 10:30 p.m.

The bomb explosion and the detritus killed people standing as far as 20 meters away from the suicide bomber and left parents and children separated in the chaos that followed.

"I went out the doors and ... saw smoke everywhere," said Natalie Sully, a teenager who attended the concert. "It was horrible."

To her right was a body, the skin peeled away to reveal nothing but flesh. Before she had a chance to register what she was seeing, there was another bang, not as loud as the other, which caused everyone around her to run in all directions in an attempt to escape.

Nick Heyward had taken his 16-year-old daughter Kaitlyn and her friend to the concert, and planned to meet them after the show at the bottom of the stairs inside the arena.

He made it to the meeting place, but when he heard the explosion, his worst fears took over.

Although he tried to keep his panic in check, "Inside, I was going crazy," he said in an interview.

When he spotted his daughter, relief washed over him, along with a feeling he hadn't experienced since the day she was born.

Security compounded the problem

In an attempt to maintain safety, security only boosted hysteria, said one survivor who told ABC News that only one exit door was open from the arena, leading to a crush of panicked teenage girls and boys frantic to get out.

"It was a recipe for disaster from the beginning," said the eyewitness, Joseph Harries, who didn't realize the extent of the injuries and fatalities until much later, as he was so focused on escaping from the arena.

"I had my best friend with me, and I grabbed hold of her wrist and told her never let go of me," he said. "We just ran. We jumped over chairs, railings to get out of the doors. We had to force open doors that wouldn't open because ... the entire capacity of the 20,000-person arena were trying to get out of one exit."

Paramedics slow to respond

According to witnesses, it took more than an hour for paramedics to arrive on the scene, and by that time, many of those who had previously been gravely injured were now dead.

Kim Dick, who was there with her husband, Phil, waiting for their own daughter, sat with one girl, who was so injured she had trouble walking, and was instead stumbling throughout the arena. Blood was pouring from her arm, her mouth and her leg, and her hair was burned.

Dick said she shouted for paramedics, but they wouldn't enter the foyer until they were certain there were no more bombs on site.

Finally, three paramedics arrived on the scene, helping injured people inside the foyer before sending them outside where more medical staff was waiting.

"Their job was to triage the injured and work with police to move people to a place close by where they could be treated safely, and where 25 paramedics were waiting in accordance with our major incident plan," the North West Ambulance Service said in a statement. "Within an hour all critical patients had been moved and were being treated by 50 paramedics. Some people had already been taken to hospital. Within four hours, all the injured that required hospital care had been transferred."

In total, 56 ambulances and seven rapid response vehicles were deployed to the incident, NWAS added.

Prime Minister responds

"We struggle to comprehend the warped and twisted mind that sees a room packed with young children not as a scene to cherish but as an opportunity for carnage," said British Prime Minister Theresa May. "These innocent, defenseless children and young people should have been enjoying one of the most memorable nights of their lives."

Instead, however, many were left severely injured or dead.

"We are working to establish the full details of what is being treated by the police as an appalling terrorist attack. All our thoughts are with the victims and the families of those who have been affected," May added.

In response, the terrorist threat level was raised to critical, the United Kingdom's highest level.

ISIS claims responsibility for attack

On May 21, the Islamic State of Iraq and the Levant took credit for the lone-wolf attack.

The bomber, 22-year-old Salman Ramadan Abedi, arrived at the ticket stall located in the arena's foyer after traveling on the Tube to Victoria Station. He waited several minutes before detonating the explosives he carried in a backpack.

While born in Manchester, Abedi was of Libyan ancestry. His family members were Libyan-born refugees who settled in the United Kingdom in order to escape the government of Muammar Gaddafi, who was internationally condemned as a dictator whose authoritarian administration violated the human rights of Libyan citizens and financed global terrorism.

According to Abedi's sister, the attack was likely in revenge for Muslim children killed by American airstrikes in Syria.

Many people who knew him, however, expressed surprise over the incident, though others were not so stunned by the news, suggesting that in most cases, someone else is aware when something wicked this way comes.

"Salman? I'm astonished by this," one member of Manchester's Libyan community said in an interview with the Guardian. He described Abedi as a quiet, respectful boy, and said his actions would likely devastate his family.

Salman Abedi and his brother Ismail worshipped at Didsbury mosque, where their father was well-known and highly regarded.

And although Abedi was a bit of a free spirit and consumed alcohol and smoked pot, both of which are against Muslim beliefs, an imam at the mosque recalled that Abedi looked at him "with hate" in 2015 after he preached against ISIS and Ansar al-Sharia, a militant group that advocated Sharia law in Libya until its demise in 2017, about a week after Abedi's attack.

That look was a warning sign that someone should have taken more seriously.

Background hints at trouble

Abedi's parents, born in Tripoli, returned to Libya in 2011 after the fall of Muammar Gaddafi, but Abedi stayed, attending Burnage Academy for Boys in Manchester between 2009 and 2011, Manchester College

67

until 2013 and the University of Salford in 2014, where he studied business management.

He dropped out to work in a bakery, and Manchester police believe he used student loans to finance the bombing plot, which included trips overseas to learn bomb-making. He had received funding for higher education as recently as April.

While British security and police were aware of some of Abedi's actions due to petty crimes, they did not consider him high risk and were unaware of his radicalized views.

However, a community worker told the BBC that he had called a hotline five years before the bombing to warn officials of Abedi's views, as well as his relationship with Islamic terrorist groups in Manchester, which he had been open enough about for him to have been banned from his mosque for extremism.

According to intelligence, Abedi made contact with members of the ISIS Battar brigade in Sabratha, Libya, where he made purchases for the construction of the bomb he used in the attack, four days before actually carrying out the plan.

Arena closed down until September

Out of respect for the dead and in order to make repairs on the facility, the Manchester Arena closed until September.

The first concert was held September 9, featuring Noel Gallagher and other acts.

Upcoming concerts include Queen with Adam Lambert, Mariah Carey, Chris Rock, Lady Gaga, Imagine Dragons and Stereophonics.

The victims

There were 22 people killed during the Manchester bombing, including:

- Georgina Callander, 18. Callander posted a picture with Grande on her social media feed. The 18-year-old was a student at Runshaw College in Leyland, about 34 miles northwest of Manchester. Before the concert, she sent a tweet to Grande: "So excited to see you tomorrow."

- Saffie Rose Roussos, 8. The youngest victim of the Manchester bombing, Roussos was described as a "beautiful little girl in every respect of the word." Saffie had attended the concert with her mother, Lisa, and her older sister, Ashlee.

- John Atkinson, 26. Atkinson was studying health and social studies at Bury College, and was leaving the stadium when the bomb went off. He was loved by many, according to posts from friends, one of whom started a GoFundMe page for his family.

- Olivia Campbell, 15. A recording of Campbell singing "On My Own" from "Les Miserables" played at the wedding of her mother, Charlotte Campbell-Hardy, and her fiancé, Paul Hodgson, just days before Campbell would have turned 16.

- Kelly Brewster, 32. Brewster, of Sheffield, died covering her niece to protect her from the explosion. Her boyfriend, Ian Winslow, announced her death on Facebook.

- Alison Howe, 45. Howe died outside the arena, where she was waiting to pick up her daughter, Darcy, from the concert, near where the bomb went off. "I can't describe the pain," said her husband, Steve Howe.

- Lisa Lees, 47. Lees was waiting with Howe for her own daughter, India, who wrote a tribute for her funeral, saying, "You were the best mum in the universe and the bestest friend that I could ask for. I will make you proud mum, I promise. I love you soooo much, more than anything and always will."

- Angelika and Marcin Klis, 40 and 42. This couple from Poland lived in York, and were killed waiting for their two daughters, Alex, 20, and Patricia.

- Martyn Hett, 29. Hett, from Stockport, a suburb of Manchester, went missing at the concert after he was separated from friends. His brother, Dan Hett, later tweeted, "They found my brother last night. We are heartbroken." Hett had appeared on the reality TV shows "Tattoo Fixers" and "Come Dine with Me."

- Nell Jones, 14. Jones was more a sister than classmate to her fellow students, said her principal, Dennis Oliver, who met with the girl's devastated parents. "I cannot imagine the loss they must feel. I have just done six assemblies to tell the pupils. Children are all over the place crying. We are all devastated. The heart wrenches for me and everyone else."

- Jane Tweddle-Taylor, 50. A school receptionist from Blackpool, a suburb of Manchester, went with a friend to the arena to pick up her friend's daughters. She was the mother of three girls, and according to her partner, Mark Taylor, "a very lovely lady, liked by everybody."

- Chloe Rutherford and Liam Curry, 17 and 19. "On the night our daughter Chloe died and our son Liam died, their wings were ready, but our hearts were not. They were perfect in every way for each other and meant to be," the families said in a joint statement. "They were beautiful inside and out to ourselves and our families, and they were inseparable. They lived to go to new places together and explore different cities. They wanted to be together forever and now they are."

- Michelle Kiss, 45. Kiss, the mother of three, was from Lancashire, and was attending the concert with her daughter. "Michelle Kiss was a loving wife to Tony, mother to Dylan,

Elliot and Millie, as well as daughter to Mick and Christine and sister to Nichola," the family said in a statement. "Family was her life and we are all obviously devastated by her loss. She has been taken away from us, and all that love her, in the most traumatic way imaginable."

- Elaine McIver, 43. McIver worked as a police officer in Cheshire, but was off duty during the concert, which she attended with her children and her partner, Paul. The rest of her family were seriously injured in the attack.

- Wendy Fawell, 50. Fawell worked at a primary school and had attended the concert with a friend and their children. Fawell's daughter, Charlotte, was taken to a hospital. "We're all devastated. Mum was a wonderful woman. She'll be sadly missed," said her son Adam Fawell in a statement.

- Eilidh MacLeod, 14. MacLeod was attending the concert as a birthday present. She had traveled from her home of Barra, an island in the Outer Hebrides off Scotland. "Words cannot express how we feel at losing our darling Eilidh," her family said in a statement.

- Sorrell Leczkowski, 14. Leczkowski, from Leeds, about 40 miles from Manchester, was attending the concert with her mother and grandmother, both of whom were injured in the explosion. "Sorrell was only 14, but she was our rock, she kept us all grounded. She was such a clever, talented, creative girl, there was nothing she couldn't do," her grandfather said in a statement.

- Megan Hurley, 15. Hurley was from Liverpool and attended the concert with her brother, who was injured in the attack. A family member, Su Benson-Carson also posted a tribute to Megan on Facebook: "So sorry to get the sad news last night, such a devastating loss ... positive thoughts to relations near and far on the loss of Megan at the Manchester concert and positive thoughts to Brad who has been seriously hurt in the attack, we are living in a mad world where nothing makes sense anymore...xx deepest thoughts go to all the family."

- Courtney Boyle, 18, and Philip Tron, 32. Both from Manchester, Tron had taken his stepdaughter Courtney to the concert. "My stunning, amazing, beautiful daughter, you were my rock. You made me so proud with all you had achieved, and my gorgeous crazy Philip, you made my world a happy place and now you are both my angels flying high in the sky," said Boyle's mother in a statement.

The aftermath

On June 4, Ariana Grande returned to Manchester to host a benefit concert, "One Love Manchester," which was free for those attending the May 22 show.

The concert–which included performances by Justin Bieber, the Black-Eyed Peas, Coldplay, Miley Cyrus, Marcus Mumford, Niall Horan, Little Mix, Katy Perry, Take That, Imogen Heap, Pharrell Williams, Robbie Williams, and Liam Gallagher–raised $13 million.

A July 9 concert was also held at New York City's The Cutting Room, featuring Broadway theatre and television performers interpreting songs by Ariana Grande.

"Death to the enemies of America. You call it terrorism, I call it patriotism. Do you hear me? Die."

– Jeremy Joseph Christian

TWO MEN DEAD AFTER HATE-FUELED STABBING ON PORTLAND TRAIN

Two men died, and one man was injured May 26 attempting to protect two teenage girls, one wearing a hijab, from being verbally assaulted by 35-year-old Jeremy Joseph Christian, a man with white supremacist ties whose beliefs were fueled by hate.

"Go home! Pay taxes! Get the fuck out! We need Americans here," Christian yelled as he drank from a bottle of sangria wrapped in a brown paper bag.

"He told us to go back to Saudi Arabia," said 16-year-old Destinee Magnum, one of the girls on the train that day. "He said we shouldn't be in his country. He was just telling us that we basically weren't anything and that we should just kill ourselves."

When they heard the words "decapitating heads," several men stepped in to attempt to calm the situation and protect the teen girls from the 250-pound vagrant with long, dirty hair who often found himself sleeping on the couches of friends.

"In the midst of his ranting and raving, some people approached him and appeared to try to intervene with his behavior and some of the people that he was yelling at," Sgt. Pete Simpson told The Oregonian in an interview. "They were attacked viciously."

In response to the three men, Christian pulled out a knife and began stabbing people, killing two men and injuring another.

"He started stabbing people and there was just blood everywhere," Magnum said, her voice catching in her throat as she remembered the attack that she and her 17-year-old Muslim friend witnessed. "We just started running for our lives."

The train was crowded, however, and they were forced to leave their belongings behind as they fled the train, which came to a stop at the Hollywood/Northeast 42nd Avenue Transit Center MAX Station.

As he departed, Christian grabbed the Muslim girl's bag, throwing it and its contents onto the highway into traffic.

Christian instigated incident

According to police, the incident began when Christian "began yelling various remarks that would best be characterized as hate speech toward a variety of ethnicities and religions," police said.

The incident echoed one from the night before, which a woman surreptitiously recorded on her phone, when Christian yelled, "Oh, it looks like we have a Christian or a Muslim fucking bus driver," he shouted. "I'll stab you, too."

The suspect stabbed three men before fleeing the train; police located him and took him into custody.

Ricky John Best, 53, a father of four and an Army veteran, died at the scene. Taliesin Myrddin Namkai-Meche, 23, a recent college graduate, died at the hospital.

Despite the attack coming just before the religious holiday of Ramadan, police weren't sure if the attack was religiously motivated.

"According to some preliminary witness statements, he was kind of spewing hate about a lot of different things," according to Portland Police Sergeant Pete Simpson. "So not specifically and exclusively anti-Muslim. ... So that's why it's hard to say at this point was he directing it at any one person, or was it just kind of in general to everyone around him. We don't know if he's got mental health issues, we don't know if he's under the influence of drugs or alcohol, or all of the above. Right now, we're in the very early stages of the investigation."

What happened on the train that day?

Video from the train as well as footage taken by train passengers captured what happened on the train.

After he was approached by the men, Christian pulled out a knife and charged at Namkai-Meche, yelling, "Do something, bitch." Fletcher stood next to Namkai-Meche and was shoved by Christian, who again yelled, "Do something."

Fletcher shoved him back and told him to get off the train. Christian responded by swinging the 3 ¾-inch folding knife he was holding, stabbing Fletcher in the neck, leaving behind a gash of several inches.

Fletcher clutched his neck to stop the bleeding and fled the train, where passengers on the platform provided first aid until police and first responders arrived to take over.

He was taken to a nearby hospital, where he was told by doctors that his wound was just millimeters away from being fatal.

Meanwhile, on the train, Christian was still using his knife, stabbing Namkai-Meche and Best, who had stepped in to help.

Chase Robinson, a passenger on the train, thought it was a fistfight, and tried to break it up.

"I go to reach out, to start pulling apart, and then I see that there's just blood everywhere," Robinson said in an interview.

With both Namkai-Meche and Best down, Christian then fled the bloody scene, still brandishing his knife, as passengers followed him to ensure that he did not get away.

He was apprehended shortly after by police, throwing his knife, which hit a police car and bounced off, but he didn't calm down, even when cuffed in the back of the patrol car.

"I just stabbed a bunch of (expletive) in their neck. ... I can die in prison a happy man," he was recorded by police video saying. "Think I stab (expletives) in the neck for fun? Oh, yeah, you're right I do. I'm a patriot. That's what liberalism gets you. I hope they all die. I'm gonna say that on the stand. I'm a patriot, and I hope everyone I stabbed died."

Namkai-Meche died at a local hospital

Stabbed in the neck twice, Namkai-Meche was on the floor of the train, a woman's tank top pressed against his neck in an effort to stop the bleeding.

"I just kept telling him, 'You're not alone. We're here,'" said Rachel Macy, who held his hand as she pressed her shirt against his skin. "'What you did was total kindness. You're such a beautiful man. I'm sorry the world is so cruel,'" she added as his blood poured out onto the floor of the train.

As he was carried away by medics, he told Macy, "Tell everyone on this train that I love them."

He later died at the hospital.

A graduate of Reed College, Namkai-Meche had studied economics and had taken a course in Islam to broaden his understanding of the world.

"My dear baby boy passed on yesterday while protecting two young Muslim girls from a racist man on the train in Portland," wrote his mother, Asha Deliverance, in a post on Facebook. "He was a hero and will remain a hero on the other side of the veil. Shining bright star, I love you forever."

His aunt also posted a tribute to the young man with the bright future who was interning at the consultancy firm the Cadmus Group.

She had been on the phone with her nephew when the incident occurred, and she heard the hate speech Christian hurled at the two young girls. She suggested Taliesin record what was happening to be used as evidence for police, but had no idea that he would put himself in harm's way to protect the two girls.

Then again, she added, that was the kind of man her nephew was.

"Taliesin was huge, just look at him, his soul didn't even fit in his body, so much love. Stop the hate, that is the message, stop the hate. He had his whole life in front of him," his aunt said

Ricky John Best stood up for his values

Ricky John Best hadn't spent 23 years in the military, fighting for his nation's freedoms, only to see them eroded by a grown man spewing hate speech at two teenage girls.

That wasn't what the father of four was about.

A former platoon sergeant for Corps maintenance who had served tours of duty in both Iraq and Afghanistan, Best retired in 2012, taking a job with the city of Portland as a technician for the Bureau of Development Services.

A resident of Happy Valley, a city of about 14,000 in Clackamas County, Oregon, Best had three teenage sons and a 12-year-old daughter, with his wife, Myhanh Best, who he met at Portland Community College.

Best was once a candidate for Clackamas County commissioner, and according to the Oregonian newspaper, refused to accept campaign donations.

He was working as an electronics repairman, a job that suited him because it allowed him to spend as much time as possible with his kids, whose life experiences he had sorely missed while serving in the military.

A third man, 21-year-old Micah David-Cole Fletcher, was severely injured in the attack.

Portland's mayor, Ted Wheeler, recognized the men for their

bravery in an interview after the attack.

"Two men lost their lives, and another was injured for doing the right thing, standing up for people they didn't know against hatred. Their actions were brave and selfless, and should serve as an example and inspiration to us all. They are heroes," Wheeler said.

Stabbing survivor struggling to cope

Micah Fletcher has had a difficult time since he was stabbed on a Portland light rail train while commuting to his place of employment.

"I got stabbed in the neck on my way to work, randomly, by a stranger I don't know, for trying to just be a nice person," said the 21-year-old, a student at Portland State University. "I don't know what to do after that, you know. I'm healing. That's what I'm doing. As much as I can, in whatever way I can."

It was inevitable, though, it seemed, that Fletcher would have intervened in the face of Christian's hate-fueled rants.

In high school, Fletcher won a citywide poetry slam for a piece speaking out against the prejudice faced by Muslims, and he still believes that healing and growth can come from the tragedy he witnessed aboard the train.

"We're about to go through a very hard time. Things are happening, the world is changing. We need to remember that this is supposed to be a city where people can be safe, where children can play, where laughter can grow and where love can take roots in the soil," he said. "It's going to take us standing together as a community if you want that to be the Portland we live in. There are a lot of different issues that we need to tackle. But we can't attack any of those issues head-on until we at least know we can be safe in our streets from violence and hatred."

For Fletcher, knowing that there were others willing to risk their lives in an attempt to fight a growing seed of discontent that is escalating not only in the United States, but also globally, was somewhat restorative, even in his grief.

"Two very good people lost their lives that day," Fletcher said. "I'm very injured, both physically and mentally. I do not feel well. And I mourn the loss of those two very brave individuals who put their lives on the line like that. I wish their families as much healing as they can in these times of immense trials and tribulations."

He also thanked those who helped him after he was stabbed, as well as those who have supported him following the incident.

Christian's violent past

According to a story appearing on CNN's website, Christian robbed a convenience store in 2002, forcing the clerk to handcuff himself to a pole while flaunting a .38-caliber revolver, before stealing cash, cigarettes and other items, according to police.

The high school dropout who later earned his GED told police he robbed the store because the clerk there "didn't sell any winning lottery tickets."

He fled the scene on his bicycle, but was shot in the head by a police officer.

He was sentenced to seven and a half years in prison for the robbery.

On Facebook, he regularly spewed hate speech, according to the Southern Poverty Law Center.

Last year, he protested the removal of a sign along an Oregon highway. "I'm sure most of you don't remember, but the American Nazi Party was taking care of a stretch of highway in Oregon about 10 years ago until ODOT took down their sign. Apparently, Nazis don't have the freedom to exercise their civic duties in this State. Why? Because we live in a Fascist Police State run by 'Liberal,' 'Multicultural' NAZIS!!!"

In a post from April 19, Christian praised Oklahoma City bomber Timothy McVeigh, writing, "May all the Gods Bless Timothy McVeigh a TRUE PATRIOT!!!"

Also in April, he attended a rally for free speech in Portland wearing a Revolutionary War-era flag. He spent the event shouting at people and was caught on video calling at least one person a nigger.

Christian's first court appearance included a verbal tirade

On May 30, during his first court appearance, Christian began ranting about the First Amendment from behind the glass partition separating him from the rest of the courtroom.

"Death to the enemies of America. Leave this country if you hate our freedom," he said. "Get out if you don't like free speech. You call it terrorism; I call it patriotism. You hear me? Die."

Current charges could end in death penalty

It has been a while since Oregon has put someone to death.

But Christian, a self-described "nihilist," (defined as a person who believes that life is meaningless and rejects all religious and moral principles), might be the one to change Oregon's history.

He dropped out of high school when he was a freshman, later earning his GED and spending a year at Portland Community College.

Now a transient who "does not know the last time he had a permanent address," Christian was booked into the Multnomah County jail and faces two counts of aggravated murder, one count of attempted murder, two counts of second-degree intimidation, being a felon in possession of a restricted weapon, as well as other charges.

The FBI is assisting Portland police in its investigation.

Renn Cannon, of the Portland FBI field office, said, "it's too early to say" if the incident will be treated as an act of domestic terrorism or a federal hate crime.

The aftermath

In a statement from its CEO, Jonathan Greenblatt, the Anti-Defamation League expressed concern over the growth of right-wing extremism in the United States.

"The deadly attack in Portland is not a rare or isolated event. Rather, this is the latest in a long string of violent incidents connected to right-wing extremists in the United States," Greenblatt said. "This consistent threat requires consistent resources and we call on our leaders to condemn this brutal act of terror and craft policy to counter all forms of violent extremism, including white supremacy."

Imtiaz Khan, the president of the Islamic Center of Portland, offered praise for the men who died while protecting the teenage girls from Christian's tirade, saying, "They really sacrificed everything. They really stood up for the values of the Constitution."

MAN WHO KEPT WOMAN CHAINED IN SHIPPING CONTAINER PLEADS GUILTY TO SEVEN COUNTS OF MURDER

A South Carolina man who held Kala Brown captive for weeks in a shipping container on a remote piece of property after killing her boyfriend has admitted to killing seven people including Brown's boyfriend, 32-year-old Charles David Carver, during a 13-year period while running one of the state's most successful real estate agencies.

Todd Christopher Kohlhepp entered the plea on May 26, less than seven months after Kala was miraculously rescued from the container where she had been "chained like a dog" and repeatedly sexually assaulted after she and her boyfriend responded to an ad for a cleaning job.

"They were going to do some work, help cleaning up the property. And he pulled out a gun and took them hostage," said Brown's friend, Daniel Herren, who said that the abduction was quick, giving the couple little time to react to the dangerous circumstances.

In fact, things went downhill almost immediately after they drove through the gates of Kohlhepp's property. The man pulled out a gun, shot and killed Charlie almost immediately, then kept Brown locked in the shipping container for months.

He had outfitted the container with dry food and other rations, and he regularly visited Brown to rape her.

Police had traced Brown's cell phone to Kohlhepp's property, a tangled maze of waist-high weeds, briars, and stands of trees with a chain-link fence surrounding it.

Authorities weren't optimistic despite social media posts on Charlie

Carver's Facebook page that would on the surface imply that the two were alive and well, at least to anyone who did not know them well.

Family members told reporters they believed Carver's profile had been hacked, and they knew something was wrong when they found that the couple's dog, a Pomeranian named Romeo, was at home alone in the apartment they shared with no food and water.

Carver's mother, Joanne Shiflet, told NBC News that the photos being posted as new were from more than a year ago, and none of the messages sounded like her son.

Prepared for the worst, police arrived at Kohlhepp's property with ATVs, a backhoe, and cadaver dogs.

They were excavating near the cargo container when they heard a desperate Brown banging on the inside of the container, alerting officers to her presence, according to Spartanburg County Sheriff Chuck Wright.

When rescued, she told them that she had watched Kohlhepp kill her boyfriend in cold blood before he hid her in the container, isolated in the woods on a large stretch of land about 80 miles from Columbia, South Carolina, a chain around her neck.

A glimpse of madness

Police filmed the rescue of Brown on November 3, 2016, and later released it.

The video begins when police, in response to Brown's screams, start breaking into the green storage container using only flashlights to guide them.

Inside, they found Brown, "chained like a dog" on a makeshift bed. She was wearing a dark, long-sleeved shirt, sweatpants and flip-flops, and her hands were cuffed uncomfortably behind her head.

"My neck's attached to the wall up here," she tells officers, who gently responded to the traumatized but composed young woman.

"We're getting bolt cutters, honey," one says.

Another asks where her boyfriend was.

Brown's response was matter-of-fact. "Charlie? He shot him. Todd Kohlhepp shot Charlie Carver three times in the chest, wrapped him in a blue tarp, put him in the bucket of the tractor, locked me down here. I've never seen him again. He says he's dead and buried. He says there are several bodies dead and buried out here."

The officers were left stunned by her response.

"She just looked at me and said, 'Thank you so much for finding me,'" said Detective Charlynn Ezell, who had combed the property in search of the missing woman and would not soon forget what she saw inside that packing crate.

"When you finally get answers, it's very emotional. I didn't know if I would ever see this girl alive," Ezell said. "When I saw Kala, that was an amazing sight. I told her mother later that it was almost as beautiful as if I were seeing my own child. To me, she was beautiful. I had cold chills."

"I think we all saw a lot of things that day that are going to stay with us," added Detective Bradley Whitfield, who broke down during the interview. "It could be anybody's child, anybody's wife or husband. I wish we could have done more."

Rescue involved hard work, lucky breaks

Still, officers did what they could to find Brown, although the actual rescue had been a long time coming.

Just two days after she disappeared, officials were able to pinpoint a ping from Brown's cell phone to the Kohlhepp property, but soon after, the cell phone's battery died.

While they sought to obtain a search warrant, the sheriff's office flew over the property, which was covered with trees, to get a lay of the land.

With a search warrant finally in hand, officers descended on the property and found the storage unit, tucked away beneath a thick stand of trees and barely visible from above.

They also found numerous guns and countless rounds of ammunition.

"It's unbelievable how much he had," one official said after finding the stash of weaponry.

In the weeks she was held, life was routine as it could be for the terrified Brown, who was fed fast food meals at 6 p.m. every day, and was occasionally allowed to walk around, although never with the chain removed.

"He told me as long as I served my purpose, I was safe," said Brown in an interview with Dr. Phil McGraw. Brown also said that her captor had bragged about how good he was at killing, and that he'd told her that he'd taken as many as 100 lives.

Jekyll and Hyde

While he did keep Brown alive in the container–one purchased thanks to a loan from his married girlfriend–Kohlhepp, a 45-year-old registered sex offender with previous kidnapping conviction, was far from an angel.

And in May, a courtroom learned just how evil the real estate mogul could be.

His sex offender status is from a 1986 kidnapping in Arizona, when the man kidnapped a 14-year-old girl, took her to his home, bound her with duct tape, and raped her repeatedly.

He served 14 years for that felony and was released in 2001.

It seems that his time in prison only made his rage more pronounced.

Kohlhepp told police that his first murders were in 2003, when the manager of Chesnee's Superbike Motorsports motorcycle store angered Kohlhepp, leading him to kill not only the owner, 30-year-old Scott Ponder, but also Ponder's mother, 52-year-old Beverly Guy, a bookkeeper there, 30-year-old service manager Brian Lucas, and 26-year-old mechanic Chris Sherbert.

It took less than seven minutes for Kohlhepp to decimate everyone in the shop the morning of November 6, 2003. The building now stands empty, a shell that reminds passersby of the devastation that occurred there and of a case that went unsolved for almost 14 years.

Ponder's friend had spoken to him just before he drove the seven-minute trip to the shop.

When he arrived, he found four people murdered where they had been standing, as if caught by surprise.

It was a carnage he would never forget.

Mechanic Chris Sherbert's body was found in the back of the shop, bent over as if he were still working on a bike. Beverly Ponder was also found in the back of the shop, and it appeared as though she was ambushed as she stepped out of the bathroom.

"Brian Lucas and Scott Ponder were both found dead. Their bodies were out here out front of the store," said Daniel Gross, a crime reporter for the Spartanburg Herald-Journal. "Except Brian's was out here closest to the sidewalk near the door there. And Scott Ponder's was closer to the parked cars here in the parking lot."

Police immediately received some valuable tips in the aftermath of the murders.

One of the last customers who had left the store that day reported seeing something strange.

"At the shop, he saw a person who had on a leather coat," said

Lorraine Lucas, Brian Lucas's mother. "It was a rather warm day and he was looking at a motorcycle. He acted like he never had any motorcycle experience."

Because of the suspicious behavior of that particular customer, police believed him to be the shooter, although it would be years before their suspect would be revealed.

While police sought the murderer, rumors swirled around regarding Chris Sherbert's potential drug connections.

Sherbert had had a court hearing the coming Monday, according to Terry Guy, Scott Ponder's stepfather. Because Sherbert was facing quite a bit of time in prison, people thought he would turn state's evidence in order to get a lighter sentence. To bolster that theory, Chris was the first person who was shot.

But the drug theory was not the only red herring for police to follow.

Scott's wife, Melissa, was pregnant when her husband died, but after the baby was born, DNA tests initially concluded that Brian, not Scott, was the father of her baby, despite adamant denials from Melissa that she'd ever been intimate with Brian.

"I said, 'We worked hard for that baby, we had to have medical procedures to have this baby, I know he's the father of my baby,'" said Melissa. "The only reasonable explanation here would be that I got the wrong baby. Those are the things you start telling yourself: Did I bring home the wrong baby from the hospital?"

She was so distraught that she stopped cooperating with the police, and considered having her husband's body exhumed in order to have another DNA test done to prove her baby's paternity.

As it happened, police had mixed up the DNA samples of both Brian and Scott at the crime scene, which caused the confusion. Of course, the damage had already been done, and it would be more than a decade, with feelings likely still bruised, before the killer confessed, sharing details of the crime scene that no one else would know.

The bike shop massacre was not Kohlhepp's only murder, however.

Two years later, he also killed 29-year-old Johnny Joe Coxie and 26-year-old Meagan Leigh McCraw-Coxie, a married couple who had been hired to do work on Kohlhepp's property.

Police were not sure why the Coxie couple ended up going anywhere with Kohlhepp, given Meagan's previous experience with the real estate agent-cum-murderer.

McCraw-Coxie had met Kohlhepp while working at the Waffle House in Roebuck, South Carolina, where Kohlhepp made the waitress so nervous that despite his being a big tipper, another woman had stepped in to ring up Kohlhepp's orders so McCraw-Coxie could limit her interactions with the man.

That initial apprehension should have kept the couple safe from harm, but apparently, Kohlhepp had made them an offer that even fear couldn't make them refuse.

McCraw-Coxie and her husband–the new parents of a baby boy– were last seen in December 2015, after McCraw-Coxie asked her mother to bail her out of jail so she and her husband could get a job.

Shortly afterwards, her mother reported her daughter and son-in-law missing.

They were never seen again, at least not until their remains were discovered on the Kohlhepp property, buried not far from the storage unit where Brown had been held.

Police believe they were murdered and buried on Kohlhepp's property soon after they disappeared.

Both bodies were fully clothed. Meagan had been shot once in the head, and her husband suffered several bullet wounds to the torso.

They were identified by tattoos and dental records after Kohlhepp led officers to the grave.

"There were some parts of the bodies we were not able to recover. But I really don't want to get into that, because there is an open investigation," Spartanburg coroner Rusty Clavenger said in a newspaper interview.

In a plea deal, Kohlhepp agreed to serve seven consecutive life terms plus 60 years on kidnapping, sexual assault, and other charges. There is no possibility of parole.

As part of his deal, the death penalty was taken off the table, although South Carolina has not executed a prisoner on death row for six years because the state does not have access to the drugs necessary to carry out a death by lethal injection.

Charges met with surprise, disbelief

Despite proof to the contrary, not everyone believed that Kohlhepp had such a dark side, which means that evil can be very easy to hide, even from people who are very, very close to that evil. (John Wayne Gacy's wife, for example, never suspected her husband was killing so many young men and burying them in the crawlspace beneath them. Too, Dennis Radar's family was shocked and horrified to learn of his arrest in the murders of ten people.)

Cherry Laurens, a real estate agent at his firm who said she had known the madman for a decade, said Kohlhepp was an outstanding, supportive boss, not at all the kind of person who would lock a woman in a storage box or bury the bodies of people he'd killed on his remote property.

In an interview, Laurens said Kohlhepp had explained away the sex offender status as a trumped-up charge from when "he had gone joyriding with a girl," upsetting her father, who was a prominent local official.

One of Kohlhepp's neighbors, who lived next door to him where he had a house in Moore, about 15 minutes from the property where Brown had been held captive, was also surprised to learn about his neighbor's sordid double life.

"Todd was–in my opinion–a likable guy," said 76-year-old Ron Owen, who called Kohlhepp private but nice to have as a neighbor.

Likeable for a serial killer, one supposes.

The hearing brings survivors to court

More than 50 family members and friends of Kohlhepp's victims spoke out during the hearing, although Kohlhepp ignored them and most of them ignored him.

One woman, however, made a point of letting the former real estate tycoon who lied about his felonies in order to obtain his license know exactly how much the murder of her loved one destroyed her family.

Cindy Coxie, whose son, Johnny, was buried on Kohlhepp's property, said that the man's 7-year-old son had spent months hoping his father was alive, waiting for him to come home, and told Kohlhepp that the worst day in her life was the one when she had to tell the boy his dad was dead.

"He hates you with his little heart," Cindy Coxie told Kohlhepp, who did not look at her as she spoke.

A survivor grows stronger

Brown did not attend the hearing, but she was satisfied with the plea deal, which she felt adequately punished the man who had killed her boyfriend and had nearly stolen her life.

She'd rather not waste any of her energy on him, anyway.

In the aftermath of her ordeal, Brown focused on her recovery, and finding her new normal after going through such a life-altering ordeal.

"She is very fragile," said her friend, Leah Miller. "We are just so grateful that she is alive, but we cannot imagine what she has witnessed and what she has endured. Kala has just got the best heart in the world. She is so loving and so trusting, and I just don't know what he must have said to her. She is kind and giving. No one deserves the horror she has experienced.

"I know that she just had to go to a place in her head and say, 'I will survive this,'" Miller added. "She's going to have to keep telling herself that every day."

Brown filed a civil suit against Kohlhepp for her two months spent in captivity and the depravity she suffered at his hands.

The aftermath

Todd Kohlhepp's case was explored in the "48 Hours" episode "Buried Truth."

In it, Kohlhepp's mother Regina Tague, in an emotional interview, insisted her son was "not a monster," and that he only murdered his victims because he had been the victim of bullying for much of his life.

"Todd is not a monster, he's not even close to it," Tague said. "He wasn't doing it for enjoyment. He was doing it because he was mad, and he was hurt."

Tague was found dead in her home in April.

Police later connected Kohlhepp's computer to a review he left for a product he'd purchased on Amazon, a shovel with a folding handle. His review was succinct and apropos for the purchase. He suggested that other users, "keep in car for when you have to hide the bodies and you left the full-size shovel at home."

He also left a review for a knife, which read, "Havnet (sic) stabbed anyone yet...... yet.... but I am keeping the dream alive and when I do, it will be with a quality tool like this..."

Girlfriend stunned and horrified

Holly Eudy was with Todd Kohlhepp for 10 years and had no idea he was a serial killer, at least not until she saw the storage container she'd purchased for him show up on the nightly news.

"It's disgusting," Eudy said in an interview with Inside Edition, adding that she "knew there was something that didn't sit right with me about him, but I couldn't really put my finger on it."

Still, it was difficult for her to break things off with the man, because Kohlhepp played on her insecurities and showered her with flattery that made her feel special.

"He gave me a lot of attention. He made me feel like I was important," she said.

It was enough to hide his true self, which could have been deadly for the woman who unwittingly helped her boyfriend create a prison for another woman.

Luckily for Eudy, Kohlhepp was caught before he had the opportunity to make her his victim as well.

Eudy could only watch in horror as Brown was transferred to the hospital after her rescue, telling the officers who were accompanying her that "some girl named Holly" was likely going to be Kohlhepp's next victim.

Police shouldn't have been surprised

In 2009, police should have been given a heads up that Kohlhepp might be dangerous.

Concerned neighbors had written to the South Carolina real estate licensing board that year after seeing Kohlhepp's Facebook profile, which was as disturbing as his Amazon reviews, and was peppered with posts about sex, guns, and revenge.

"Something MUST be done to stop this crazy man before something dreadful happens," they wrote in the letter.

It's no wonder his neighbors were concerned.

His Facebook posts read: "Serial killers need love too" and "reading the news … this person missing, that person missing, another person missing–oh wait–that person just went to beach with friend, another person found with her parole violation boyfriend... In the event I become missing, please note that no one would take me. I eat too much and I am crabby, they would just bring me back or give me 20 bucks for a cab ride. Most likely if I am missing, it is because my dumb ass did something on the tractor again and I am too stubborn to go to the doctor... I got nine lives... I ain't done yet."

Unfortunately for everyone, however, he was only getting started.

Kohlhepp obtained his real estate license in 2006, a full three years after the motorcycle shop murders.

When he applied for his license, he had to explain away a 15-year prison sentence for kidnapping a 14-year-old girl at gunpoint.

Kohlhepp, who was 15 at the time, was convicted of kidnapping and rape after holding the girl hostage in his bedroom.

MISSISSIPPI SHOOTING LEAVES 8 DEAD, INCLUDING A DEPUTY

Apparently, 35-year-old Willie Corey Godbolt has a tough time controlling his temper.

Even his pastor, Rev. Eugene Edwards, thought the man was out of control.

Edwards told The New York Times that he had known Godbolt for about 19 years and said he had a "very bad temper."

But nothing could explain the carnage that occurred at the end of May, sparked by an argument with his estranged wife and her family.

On May 27, he gunned down eight people in a multi-house spree killing in rural Mississippi, including a deputy, over an argument with his estranged wife over their children.

"I ain't fit to live, not after what I done," Godbolt, 35, told The Jackson Clarion-Ledger as he sat along the side of the road, his hands cuffed behind his back. "My intention was to have God kill me. I ran out of bullets."

The incident began just before midnight on the night of May 27, when a deputy responded to a domestic disturbance call at a home near Brookhaven, a community about 70 miles south of Jackson.

The call was regarding an argument between Godbolt, his estranged wife, and her family over the custody of the couple's two children.

"He'd come to get his kids. The deputy was called," said Vincent Mitchell, Godbolt's stepfather-in-law.

The deputy asked Godbolt to leave, and Mitchell thought he was going to comply with the officer's orders.

In an interview, Mitchell said that Godbolt made the motions of a person who was planning to leave, then suddenly "reached in his back pocket and grabbed a gun. He just started shooting everything."

Although domestic cases are commonplace for the Lincoln County Sheriff's Department, this time was different.

"At some point, it went really bad," Lincoln County Sheriff Steve Rushing said.

Almost immediately after everyone believed the situation was under control, gunfire erupted, eventually spreading between three homes as Godbolt fled one scene, switched vehicles, and went to another to continue his rampage. After the shooting was over, eight people were dead, including the sheriff's deputy who had responded to the call and two young boys.

According to Godbolt, the situation began peacefully but quickly escalated.

"I was having a conversation with her stepdaddy and her mama and her, my wife, about me taking my children home," he said.

The conversation must have grown heated, because, according to Godbolt, one of the neighbors called 911, a move that he blames for the ensuing death of the deputy.

"They cost him his life," he said of the deputy. "My pain wasn't designed for him. He was just there. I'm sorry."

Godbolt had intended to die

According to one of the survivors, Vincent Mitchell, Godbolt's wife and two children were staying at his Bogue Chitto home–a community with just over 500 people–and had been there for about three weeks, ever since she left Godbolt.

Although the arrival of the sheriff's deputy initially appeared to diffuse the situation, and Godbolt seemed ready to leave, he instead pulled a gun from his back pocket and opened fire.

Mitchell escaped along with Godbolt's wife, Sheena, but said that his wife, Barbara Mitchell, her daughter, Toccarra May, and his wife's sister, Brenda May, were killed in his home.

"I'm devastated. It don't seem like it's real," Mitchell said outside his yellow frame house, set amid a neighborhood of similarly modest homes, trailer homes, and small churches, all surrounded by thick woods. "Him and my stepdaughter, they've been going back and forth for a couple of years with that domestic violence."

About a year before the shooting, Sheena Godbolt had taken out a restraining order against her husband, accusing him of felony domestic violence. In court papers, she said he had punched her in the stomach more than once, had choked her and had held his hand over her mouth, preventing her from screaming.

Godbolt said that once 911 had been called and the officer was on the scene, he intended for the slain deputy, 36-year-old William Durr, to take his life.

"Suicide by cop was my intention," Godbolt said.

Durr had served two years in the sheriff's department and had previously worked as a Brookhaven police officer. The married father of an 11-year-old son worked as a ventriloquist when he was off duty and often volunteered at schools and churches, because he loved to perform for children.

"He had a heart of gold," Lincoln County Sheriff Steve Rushing said. "He loved doing anything with kids. He would go out of his way to help anybody."

After fleeing the initial crime scene, Godbolt killed four more people at two other homes.

He was arrested about seven hours after the first shooting near the final crime scene in a subdivision in Brookhaven, a few miles from Bogue Chitto.

Two boys were found dead at another home, 11-year-old Austin Edwards and 18-year-old Jordan Blackwell.

"While we were consoling his wife's family, he was at my sister's home, killing our children, my son, and my sister's son," said Sheila Edwards.

There were multiple children at the home where Austin and Jordan had died. They had received a call from the Bogue Chitto home, warning them about Godbolt and telling them to lock the door.

The boys did as they were told and secured the door, but it hadn't done much good. Godbolt shot and kicked in the door to gain entry to the home.

According to Caleb Edwards, Austin's brother and Jordan's cousin, the boys were playing a game in the house, and heard one shot. Initially, they thought it was a firecracker.

That shot was likely the one fired by Godbolt as he attempted to gain entry to the house.

The boys–almost a dozen children were at the house at the time of the incident–then heard multiple gunshots, and they ran pell-mell in an attempt to seek safety.

According to Edwards, Godbolt asked Jordan where his parents were, and when Jordan said they weren't home, Godbolt "just started shooting."

(Jordan's parents had left to go to the scene of the first shooting, after receiving a call from Godbolt's estranged wife, Sheena. "When she called me, she told me something had happened, and somebody had gotten shot. I told my husband and my sister and my other friend who was here, 'I need to go be with Sheena,'" said Tiffany Blackwell.)

Jordan used his own body to shield his cousin from the bullets.

"He loved me enough to take some bullets for me," said Caleb, adding that he felt the force of the bullets that lodged in his cousin's body as he crouched beneath him. "I thought I was going to die."

Godbolt's wife's sister and her brother-in-law, 45-year-old Ferral Burage, and his wife, 46-year-old Shelia Burage, were found dead at the third house.

"It breaks everybody's heart," said Garrett Smith, a 19-year-old college student who had attended high school with one of the victims. "Everybody knows everybody for the most part."

Tiffany Blackwell found her son and his cousin after the murders.

"When I walked in the house and saw my child lying there, I just thought he was sleeping," she said. "I told him to wake up. I told him to get up, but he wouldn't move."

Jordan Blackwell, who dreamed of getting a Camaro for his high school graduation, according to his mother, Tiffany Blackwell, was a linebacker for the Brookhaven High School football team, and although he was just a rising senior, two universities and a nearby community college had already expressed interest in adding him to their teams.

It was an honor Jordan deserved, said Trace Clopton, who played football with Jordan Blackwell, recalling his friend's character.

"He was always thinking of others," said Clopton. "He was selfless."

Jordan's father, Shon Blackwell, said he was relieved that Godbolt wasn't killed during the incident.

"I'm glad he didn't die. He needs to understand what he did," he said. "I want him to wake up every morning and know what he's done. First thing in the morning. I just want to ask him, 'Why my son, why Austin?' I want to look him in his face and say, 'Why the two kids, what purpose?'

"I never would have thought in a million years that he would hurt the kids," he added. "He mentored both of them. They looked up to him. ... That's the part that hurts. That's the part that penetrates you."

Mississippi Gov. Phil Bryant asked for prayer after the murder spree, and praised the deputy for his courage.

"Every day, the men and women who wear the badge make some measure of sacrifice to protect and serve their communities. Too often, we lose one of our finest. I thank the law enforcement agencies involved for their hard work," Bryant said.

Godbolt had a long criminal history

According to the Brookhaven Daily Leader, Godbolt's criminal history dates back more than a decade.

His previous charges include:

- Armed robbery and aggravated assault in 2005, after he allegedly pistol-whipped a man and took his cash and jewelry.
- Simple assault, a 2013 charge filed by the Lincoln County Sheriff's Office.
- Disorderly conduct, breach of peace and failure to comply with a request from a sheriff, which led to his arrest in 2015.
- Also in 2015, Godbolt was arrested by the Mississippi Highway Patrol for speeding, driving with a suspended license and no proof of insurance.

Godbolt was arrested at a nearby gas station after leaving on foot from the last home where the shooting took place. He had also been shot, likely by someone firing in self-defense at one of the homes. Godbolt faces one count of capital murder in the death of deputy Durr and seven counts of first-degree murder in the deaths of the extended family members.

He was denied bond during his first court appearance on May 30. The judge said he would be appointed a lawyer.

District attorney Dee Bates declined to speculate on what charges Godbolt might face.

Based on the number of murders, however, when his case goes to trial, Godbolt could get his final wish of death.

If found guilty, he could receive the death penalty or life without the possibility of parole for the capital murder charge.

Of note

About a year before the shooting spree, Godbolt posted a Bible verse on his Facebook page, James 4:7, which reads, "Submit yourself, then, to God. Resist the devil and he will flee from you."

June

TERRORISTS KILL EIGHT
IN LONDON ATTACK

At about 10 p.m. on June 3, 2017, a van carrying three Islamic terrorists left the road in London, England, striking several pedestrians on London Bridge.

After the van crashed, the three men fled the vehicle and began terrorizing unsuspecting people who were relaxing at nearby restaurants and pubs.

The attackers were later shot dead by police, but not before killing eight people and wounding another 48.

They were wearing fake suicide vests fashioned from water bottles and duct tape to make themselves even more imposing, a tactic that was designed to create "maximum fear" for anyone encountering the men, according to Commander Dean Haydon of the London Metropolitan Police.

"Anyone who saw them on the night would have thought they were genuine," he said. "It is hard to speculate what the motive was for wearing the belts. It could be that they had plans to take the attack into a siege situation, or it might be that they saw it as protection from being shot themselves.

Still, the belts made the reactions of both the people and the public all the more courageous, because there was no way for them to know that they were not at risk of being injured or killed in an explosion.

The scene was chaotic, witnesses said.

"They went 'This is for Allah,' and they had a woman on the floor. They were stabbing her," witness Gerard Vowls said.

Florin Morariu, a chef working at a nearby bakery, said he watched two of the attackers stabbing one of the victims.

Initially, he stood frozen, in shock over what he saw and unsure of how to respond. He then used a bread basket to hit one of the attackers over the head before police threw a grenade into the crowd, creating enough chaos that Morariu could get away.

"Then I ran," the chef said.

The victims

People from around the world were among the victims killed in the terror attack.

They include:

- Ignacio Echeverría, 39. Echeverría was from Spain, and worked at HSBC in London. He was killed when he saw the incident unfold while skateboarding in the park, and stopped to confront one of the assailants. His family confirmed his death on social media.

- Alexandre Pigeard, 26. Pigeard was French, but was working as a waiter at a restaurant near Borough Market, where much of the carnage took place. According to Vincent Le Berre, a bartender at the restaurant, staff there had undergone terrorist attack training two days prior to the attack. Le Berre acted quickly and he was able to save 40 customers, but did not have enough time to save Pigeard as well.

- Sara Zelenak, 21. Zelenak was from Australia and was in

London working as an au pair. She attempted to flee her attackers while in Borough Market, where she had been out with friends on a rare night off from work, but was unsuccessful. Zelenak's aunt called her "the girl next door," in an interview with the BBC.

- Kirsty Boden, 28. Another Australian, Boden was working in London as a nurse, and according to her family, ran toward the danger when she saw people were injured. "We are so proud of Kirsty's brave actions which demonstrate how selfless, caring, and heroic she was, not only on that night, but throughout all of her life," they said in a statement.

- Chrissy Archibald, 30. Archibald, a native of British Columbia, was working at a homeless shelter at the time of her death, in the arms of her fiancé, Tyler Ferguson, on London Bridge. She and Ferguson had been living in the Netherlands while Ferguson wrapped up an overseas contract.

- James McMullan, 32. McMullan, a native of Great Britain, was living in London at the time of his death. "While our pain will never diminish, it is important for us to all carry on with our lives in direct opposition to those who are trying to destroy us and remember that hatred is the refuge of small-minded individuals and will only breed more," McMullan's sister, Melissa McMullan, said in an interview with Sky News. "This is not a course we will follow despite our loss."

- Sebastien Belanger, 36. Belanger was a French national working in London as a chef who had gone out for a drink with friends after watching a soccer match when he was killed.

- Xavier Thomas, 45. The body of Thomas, a French national, was found four days after the attack in the Thames River. He had been thrown off London Bridge when the van struck the milling pedestrians and had been swept up by the current. Thomas was walking with his girlfriend, Christine Delcros, at the time of the attack. She was seriously injured but is expected to make a full recovery.

Police make more arrests after short investigation

The area was on lockdown for 24 hours following the attack. Police arrested ten more people in the east London neighborhood of Barking after determining that two of the terrorists responsible for the attack lived in that neighborhood.

According to reports, police killed the men responsible for the attack eight minutes after it began.

Eight officers fired some fifty rounds, said Assistant Commissioner Mark Rowley, the head of counter-terrorism for London Metropolitan Police Service.

ISIS claimed responsibility shortly after the attack.

In the van involved in the crash, police found thirteen wine bottles filled with flammable liquid and wrapped in rags, two blow torches, office chairs and a suitcase, believed to be part of the men's cover story, and bags filled with gravel, thought to be cover for the men.

A FIRED EMPLOYEE SEEKS REVENGE

In April, 45-year-old John Robert Neumann Jr. was fired from his job at an Orlando awning company, one of the largest manufacturers of awnings for camper vans, SUVs, and motor coaches.

He had worked there for several years, and he didn't go quietly.

For the next two months, Neumann plotted revenge. On Monday, June 5, he returned to his former workplace Fiamma, Inc.–a factory the size of two Florida Gators' football fields–and killed five former co-workers before taking his own life as the sound of sirens approached from a distance.

According to police, the disgruntled former employee had spent time planning the shooting before returning to his former place of employment to seek revenge for his firing, and to make anyone who may have played a role in it pay dearly.

"He shot five innocent people and then turned the gun on himself and killed himself," said Orange County Sheriff Jerry Demings, who did not share why Neumann might have lost his job.

The scene was surreal

Neumann entered the cavernous building through a rear door, gun in hand. He was also carrying two knives, one a large hunting knife.

One of the first people he encountered, a woman who had been hired after Neumann was let go, was able to flee the building and ran across the street to a tile business in order to call 911.

"All she kept saying was he was holding a gun and told her to get out," said Yamaris Gomez, the owner of the tile store and the first to learn what had happened at the business on the other side of the road.

Both state and federal police arrived at the industrial park just after 8 a.m., alerted by the call, but by then, Neumann's carnage was complete.

Five of his former co-workers were dead from gunshots to the head, including one co-worker he'd previously had a negative relationship with.

According to Demings, while the actual motive for the shooting was unclear, it was evident that he was singling out victims during the shooting.

Seven other workers, including the woman who'd escaped across the street, were in the building at the time, but were unharmed in Neumann's calculated act of revenge.

Neumann had paused once to reload, and as he heard the sirens in the background, took his own life rather than face the consequences of his actions.

Those killed were 69-year-old Robert Snyder, 44-year-old Brenda Montanez-Crespo, 53-year-old Kevin Clark, 57-year-old Jeffrey Roberts, and 46-year-old Kevin Lawson.

One of the survivors was in the ladies' restroom when she heard a loud bang, and exited the bathroom to find someone lying on the floor.

The first person she called was her sister, Shelly Adams, who later relayed the resulting phone call to a local television station.

"She was very distraught," Adams said regarding the cell phone call. "She just kept saying, 'I'm OK, I'm OK, my boss is dead, my boss is dead.' She was very, very upset. It's unbelievable that this could happen in a small business."

The woman was not injured in the episode of workplace violence but went into shock afterward due to what she had seen happen during the deadly shooting.

Not the first on-the-job incident between police and Neumann

In 2014, police had visited the factory after a co-worker reported Neumann for assault.

According to Demings, police were called over an incident of battery, but no charges were filed at the time.

According to the 2014 incident report, the co-worker had initially told police that Neumann punched him in the back of the head, knocking him to the ground. He later changed his story, and said Neumann had chased him first and then hit him in the back of the head.

The co-worker, who had had no visible injuries when interviewed by officers, told police that he had had issues in the past with Neumann but thought they had been resolved.

That co-worker was not one of the victims in the shooting.

Neumann had long police record

Neumann had a record of minor crimes dating back more than 20 years, most of them traffic incidents–driving with a suspended license, driving under the influence, giving a deputy a false name and leaving the scene of a hit and run–as well as possession of marijuana, but none of them were violent, and none of them were recent.

Neumann was a veteran who had received an honorable discharge from the U.S. Army in 1999. He did not have a concealed weapons permit, authorities said.

Neumann's life outside the factory

Neumann lived in a trailer park in nearby Maitland, surrounded by a funeral home, a used car lot, and a dog-grooming business.

Neighbors said he, like many mass shooters, kept to himself.

According to one neighbor, Arnie Boyd, Neumann rode his bike around the trailer park now and again, but the two rarely spoke, and if they did, conversations never got too personal.

Neumann was divorced and lived alone and has no family in the area.

According to Demings, there were no outward signs that Neumann planned to kill his coworkers that day and no one had reported any suspicious activity on Neumann's part.

"This violence is frustrating," Demings said. "The only way we have a fighting chance is to ask the public to report any suspicious activity."

One neighbor did have an idea that something may not have been quite right with Neumann, who had anger issues and seemed to be the type who brooded over things that went wrong in his life.

"It just seemed like there was something always bothering him," the neighbor said, adding that his brooding nature did not improve after he was fired from Fiamma Inc. in April, a situation he declined to talk about.

Timing was particularly tragic

The event came almost a year after the shooting at the Pulse nightclub in Orlando, which at the time was the deadliest shooting in modern U.S. history. It left 49 dead and 58 people injured. Pulse's unwelcome record has since been overtaken by the Las Vegas shooting, which left 58 people dead and 546 injured.

"Over the past year, the Orlando community has been challenged like never before," Florida Governor Rick Scott said in a statement. "I ask all Floridians to pray for the families impacted by this senseless act of violence."

A BOYFRIEND GETS A TERRIBLE SURPRISE

Dale Kostar was just stopping by to visit his girlfriend at about 8 p.m. on June 11.

She had been expecting him, so when she didn't come to the door in response to his knocking, he picked the lock and went inside the family home.

Inside, Koster was horrified to find his girlfriend, Taylor Pifer, dead, along with her mother and sister, at the 11400 block of Ridge Road, in North Royalton, Ohio, just south of Cleveland.

When he found the bodies, he called 45-year-old Suzanne Taylor's boyfriend, Scott Plymale, who immediately made a call to 911.

"[Kostar] said they didn't open the door, he picked the lock and went in, and he said the bedroom door is closed and opened the bedroom door and he said there's a body in here," said Plymale.

Plymale also told the 911 dispatcher that he had left flowers at the house on Saturday, but saw no one inside at that time. The bouquet he'd left was still outside the home on Sunday when police arrived.

According to the girls' stepmother, Sonya Pifer, Taylor, 21, attended Kent State University–infamous for a National Guard shooting during a political protest that left four students dead in 1970–and Kylie, 18, was a student at Bowling Green State University, also in Ohio.

Taylor was majoring in fashion design, while Kylie was majoring in forensic science, Pifer said.

The girls were estranged from their father since adulthood, she said.

According to police, all three women were found dead in one of the home's bedrooms, although the daughters appeared to have been moved to the mother's bedroom after being killed elsewhere in the home.

"A knife was used in one death. I cannot tell you on the others because there's not a visible sign of how death occurred," said North Royalton Detective Dave Loeding, adding that the three bodies were under covers, almost as if they'd been tucked into bed.

Later, police revealed that Suzanne Taylor's throat was slashed. According to investigators, Kylie Pifer was strangled with a phone cord and Taylor Pifer was smothered with a pillow.

Friends mourn deaths

"I can't think of anyone who would want to do this to such a gorgeous family at all," said Emma Davis, a friend of both Taylor and Kylie Pifer.

Taylor, she said, was a "girly girl" who loved to play dress up when they were children, and later, used her childhood imagination to start making her own clothes and doing makeup.

Kylie, on the other hand, was more interested in science, and loved watching the shows "CSI" and "Bones," although she also loved drama and spent plenty of time working behind the scenes of North Royalton High School productions.

"She was so bright and so bubbly," Davis said. "She was an all-around, nonjudgmental person, so when she walked in a room and someone made her laugh or smile it was like everyone in the room noticed. She was just such a genuine person in almost anything that she did."

Both girls also played soccer and softball as children.

Davis's mother Samantha Goliat, coached Kylie in soccer and was having trouble processing the crime.

"I can see people going off the deep end and doing whatever it is they do but not to them, not to these girls. It just doesn't make any sense," she said. "This is just wrong...just wrong. Snuffed out two beautiful girls' lives and they haven't really started living them yet, it's just not right."

According to police, the women were alive Saturday afternoon and were killed sometime that evening.

A motive for the killings remains unclear, but police said the case does not involve a suicide. So far, no arrests have been made.

Case might have gone cold if not for second murders

On Sunday, while police were converging on the North Royalton home Suzanne Taylor shared with her daughters, George Brinkman Jr. was house sitting for some friends in neighboring Stark County.

Rogell "Gene" John, 71, and his wife, Roberta "Bobbi" John, 64, had been on vacation and had asked Brinkman to keep an eye on their home.

They were shot to death on Sunday evening in the master bedroom of their home.

According to Stark County Sheriff George Maier, the bodies were found in their North Canton home on Monday after a son grew concerned when he was unable to reach them after they'd returned from their vacation.

When his father didn't show up for work that day, the son drove from his Mount Vernon home to check on things. After looking inside the home, he called 911, telling the operator that the things they'd taken on vacation "were still by the stairs," and that the dog was barking.

As in the North Royalton case, the couple were both in bed, with blankets covering them, although the son reported seeing his stepmother's leg sticking out from beneath a blanket.

Brinkman had previously dated the couple's daughter, according to news reports.

According to neighbors, the couple had been in the neighborhood of one- and two-story houses for decades and were nice but kept to themselves, according to 24-year-old Taylor Brown, who lived next door to the Johns' in North Canton, Ohio.

Brown said he saw Brinkman visiting their home a few times, and neighbors reported seeing his black van at the home near the time of the deaths.

Search for suspect results in standoff

With the help of the FBI, which was able to track Brinkman's cell phone, he was found at the home of a woman in Brunswick who he had contacted looking for a place to stay, according to North Royalton Detective Dave Loeding. Both the woman and her daughter were at the home when authorities tracked him there about an hour later and made contact, which resulted in a nine-hour standoff.

During the standoff, Brinkman casually held a Facebook conversation with a TV reporter, telling her that he'd known the women in North Royalton for a long time.

Brinkman had also known the Johns for a long time, and they evidently trusted him enough to allow him to house-sit for them and care for their aging dog while they were on vacation.

Hoping for a peaceful resolution, police negotiated with Brinkman through a window then entered the home through an unlocked front door and took him into custody using a Taser.

Police questioning neighbors in the days following the North Royalton murders learned that a black van had been seen at the home around the time of the killings, Loeding said, adding that Brinkman's name was mentioned as "somebody who visits once in a while."

Brinkman faces the death penalty

According to the Cuyahoga County Prosecutor's Office, it would seek the death penalty in the deaths of Suzanne Taylor and her daughters.

Brinkman is currently being held in Cuyahoga County on a $75 million bond.

Couple sentenced to death for horrific abuse of child

Because they weren't sure who her father was, Ame Deal was the scapegoat in her family.

And because of it, she suffered the most at the hands of her abusive family, who seemed to enjoy the torture they inflicted regularly on the 10-year-old girl with the blond hair, bright blue eyes, and an impish, shy smile.

In abusive households, sometimes there is one child singled out to suffer more than all the rest.

According to experts, it is a way for families in crisis to put blame somewhere other than where it truly belonged, like brushing toast crumbs underneath a kitchen rug.

"Scapegoating is often a way for families to hide problems that they cannot face," according to Dr. Allan Schwartz, Ph.D., a licensed clinical social worker. "In the examples of cases I have worked with one or both parents were abusive to their children. In adulthood, scapegoating became a way for adult children to hide the fact of family history of abuse by blaming everything on one member who seemed vulnerable for attack. In that way, the less favored sibling becomes the repository of everything that is wrong in the family."

In her household, the scapegoat was 10-year-old Ame Deal, who died in 2011, just two weeks before her 11th birthday, after spending a night padlocked in a plastic box in a sizzling garage in Arizona when temperatures didn't dip below 95 degrees at night.

Before Ame was squeezed into the trunk, however, she was forced to do jumping jacks and backbends, and to run around in 103-degree heat for more than an hour. Then the trunk was padlocked shut, to prevent Ame from using her feet to hold open the lid enough to get some air to pass through so she could breathe in the oven that would soon enough become her tomb.

The reason?

She'd taken a Popsicle out of the freezer without asking to cool off from the heat.

At least, that's what someone said she'd done.

She might have, seeing as how she weighed less than 60 pounds, and was never fed the same amount of food as the other kids, leaving her feeling hungry all the time. But maybe she didn't.

Either way, it was an opportunity for Sammantha and John Allen–both sentenced to death this year for their roles in Ame's prolonged murder–to torture the girl who was the household scapegoat.

None of the other children in the home were ever punished, if what happened to Ame Deal can be considered punishment. Sadism seems a more appropriate word for what the child was forced to endure.

Not her first time in the box

It was not the first time Ame had been in the box.

John Allen said he had locked the girl in the box about ten times or so before, despite there being little air in the box, making it devastatingly dangerous in the sweltering Arizona heat.

He knew how dangerous it was, the 31-by-12-by-14-inch plastic locker with latches to secure the lid, and a padlock just to make sure there was no chance to escape.

Ame was 48 inches tall, so she had to curl her body up in order to fit in inside.

While that alone would be excessive punishment for most people, the box alone usually wasn't enough for the Allens.

Sometimes, John Allen would roll or throw the box around the garage while Ame was in it. Sometimes they would throw the box into the swimming pool, a deranged version of waterboarding that likely left the girl terrified of water.

Occasionally, Cynthia Stoltzmann, Ame's aunt on her father's side and her legal guardian, would sit on the box, listening to her niece cry inside.

Usually, John Allen said, when she was allowed out of the box, she was sweaty and weak but "not fainting, not out of it," he told police.

As far as anyone in that household was concerned, Ame deserved it.

"Ame lies. Ame steals. Ame needs to be punished," family members later told police.

And punished she was.

In addition to the box, Ame was also punished with paddling, by being forced to eat dog poop when hot sauce on her tongue became a treat, being forced to walk barefoot on asphalt when the heat rose so high that the surface likely blistered her skin, or being positioned on her hands and feet, her back arched, holding the pose until she collapsed in pain, only to be put back in it again.

Ame was a scapegoat all right. And she paid for it with her life.

A deadly family tree

Ame Lynn Deal was born on July 24, 2000, in Monongahela, Pennsylvania, the daughter of Shirley and David Deal, although Shirley was having an affair at the time of Ame's conception and she was never quite sure if Ame was David's daughter or the other man's, Kenny Griest. David Deal insisted she wasn't his daughter, and based on photographic evidence, Griest would have loved to

115

have her. Still, Deal is listed as the father on Ame's birth certificate.

Shirley left David, with whom she had already had two other children, after Ame was born, and the little family moved in with her mother while she tried to make a relationship work with Griest. For some reason, she and her three children followed David to Midland, Texas, away from any of Shirley's family, in an attempt to reunite with David. Shirley and her brood moved in with David's mother, Judith, and his sister, Cynthia Stoltzmann, but the two women hated her for having an affair. According to Shirley, the family took their anger out on her but not the kids, and they hit her and called her names until they finally forced her out of the house, refusing to allow her to take the kids.

Shirley moved to Kansas and left Ame and the other children behind. But everyone knew that Ame might not be David Deal's real daughter. That bit of information, the fact that Ame might not have been a blood relative, made all the difference when it came to the rest of Ame's short, tragic life.

The Deals, who had already moved from Pennsylvania to Texas, continued to bounce from state to state, including Minnesota and Utah, until they ended up in Arizona.

The family home-schooled the kids and kept to themselves, likely because they weren't really homeschooling anyone, and housekeeping wasn't a priority.

In every state they lived, the family lived in dirty, derelict homes that gathered cockroaches and rodents like snowflakes fall in winter. These were not places where visitors would feel very welcome.

In Utah, the state investigated the family for possible child abuse, but they'd moved on before anything could be done to protect the children, and the suspicions didn't follow them when they left the state.

By the time they'd arrived in Arizona, Ame was Sammantha Allen's responsibility, despite Sammantha having stopped any pretense of homeschooling sometime around the fourth grade. The place was Sammantha's 20th home in 18 years.

"Her world was small and very isolated, and it was dominated by her family," said her defense attorney, John Curry. "That's all she knew. That's all she knew."

Everyone failed Ame

Neighbors noticed Ame being forced to walk barefoot on hot pavement and recognized the fear in her eyes.

They also saw her with dog feces being smeared on her face when she failed to miss a bit when cleaning up after the family pets outside, and crushing aluminum cans with her tender bare feet.

They also heard screaming coming from the plastic locker when John Allen kicked it around the yard.

But they didn't call police until about a week before Ame's death, and when they did, that call had nothing to do with the abuse Ame suffered at the hands of her so-called family.

The call was about children throwing rocks in the neighborhood.

Officer Albert Salaiz was the one who took the call, and he dispersed the children.

He didn't notice anything out of the ordinary that day, although now, he wracks his brain trying to remember if he missed something he should have seen, failed to recognize someone's silent cries for help.

The day after

It was 8 a.m. the next morning before anyone opened the box to let Ame out and end her punishment.

When they did, she wasn't moving, she wasn't breathing. At some time during the night, she'd wet herself, something that she likely feared would earn another punishment, if she wasn't already dead when it happened. (Another favorite punishment for Ame was being forced to sleep on the shower floor on nights she wet the bed, although that would have been cool, refreshing comfort compared to the hell that was that box.

Still, it was at least a half an hour later before anyone bothered to call 911.

Salaiz was first on the scene and arrived to find a home with used tampons on the floor, the acrid scent of dried blood and stale urine filling the space.

Ame was twisted unnaturally and beginning to go into the early stages of rigor mortis, making her position, arms bent as though she was trying to press open the top of the plastic tub, even more distressing. Her lips were the same blue as the dirty carpet she was laying on.

"I never, to this day, will forget what she looked like. That image is ingrained on my mind," Salaiz said.

John Allen was standing next to Ame while a paramedic attempted CPR, even though the girl was clearly already dead and had been for some time.

They were talking about a game of hide and seek, and attempted to say that Ame had locked herself in the box accidentally.

"There was no emotion from him or the grandma either. That's what bothered me. There was no emotion," Salaiz said. "I'd never seen anything like that."

Later, the officer asked John Allen for a statement, while Allen relaxed on a swing outside, swinging gently back and forth as if everything was completely normal in his world and a little girl wasn't dead, Salaiz said.

Allen told the officer that he and Sammantha had gone to bed at about 1 a.m., leaving Ame, a 12-year-old girl, and their three-year-old daughter playing hide-and-seek, well past a reasonable bedtime.

In the morning, they'd found Ame locked in the box, assumed the game had gone awry, and called 911.

They blamed John and Sammantha's three-year-old, said she loved to lock things up and run away. Everyone in the house had the story down, especially since John Allen had written down what he thought everyone should say on a page in a spiral notebook.

"Ame found passed away in box. They (the kids) were playing hide-and-go-seek. We believe she fell asleep and suffocated," he wrote.

Salaiz didn't believe that they would have left a three-year-old unsupervised, but everyone told him the same story, including the 12-year-old.

"She said, 'Yeah, they found Ame dead,' and she keeps walking past me," Salaiz said. One critical detail of her story was off, however. The 12-year-old said she'd gone to bed at 9 p.m., which Salaiz believed to be more truthful than the adults allowing a three-year-old to stay awake past midnight without adult supervision.

"I felt the 12-year-old ... knew what happened. She knew about the box," Salaiz said.

Back at the station, Salaiz's sergeant asked him about the call.

"I told my supervisor, 'They fucking killed her.' He got pissed. 'You can't be saying that. You don't know that for a fact,'" Salaiz said.

But Salaiz knew the truth; he knew it was a fact. He'd seen all the evidence he needed at the home where Ame Deal had died. That knowledge would haunt him for the rest of his life.

The Maricopa County Medical Examiner's Office determined that Ame had suffered from heat exhaustion and dehydration before dying of asphyxiation, and the case was ruled a homicide.

A week later, the adults in the home–Ame's legal guardian, Cynthia Stoltzmann, Ame's father, David Deal, Ame's grandmother, Judith Deal, Ame's cousin, Sammantha Allen and Sammantha's husband, John–had been arrested in association with Ame's horrifying death.

"This child died at the hands of those who were supposed to love and care for her ... this case has turned the stomachs of some of our most seasoned detectives," Phoenix police spokesperson Sergeant Trent Crump said.

At least a dozen other children who lived at the home were placed with Child Protective Services.

Attempt at cover-up fails

But still, John Allen tried to hide what had truly happened to Ame, though he was caught because he had forgotten that conversations had in a police station are anything but private.

"We should have come up with something very solid, all together as a family, and nobody would have to take the fall," John told his wife in an interview room, unaware police were recording everything that was being said.

Eventually, John Allen told the story, weaving it in such a way that it was clear he was trying to cover for his wife.

"It should have been me," he said.

Public turns on child welfare agency

As details of Ame's death went public, people were outraged and wondered how Ame had fallen so deeply between the cracks, especially given the squalid conditions of the home in which she had lived.

Officer Salaiz struggled to remember what he had noticed when he had been called a week before Ame died about the rock-throwing incident, and found himself wracked with guilt, despite the lack of signs.

"I'm going through my mind: Why didn't I see something? Why didn't I notice something? I beat myself up. You have no idea. That was my area that I patrolled every day," Salaiz said. "People were coming out of the woodwork to tell stories of abuse at that house. That upset me even more because why didn't anybody pull me over on the beat and tell me?"

For Salaiz, the case of Ame Deal changed everything, and his happiness was replaced with morose gloom despite counseling.

"That case changed my life. It took some of the joy out of life for me," said Salaiz, who retired for medical reasons three years after Ame's death. "I wasn't the same person. I'm still not. I'd wake up and say, 'What's my purpose? Why am I here?' I failed."

Juries hand down sentences

Justice for Ame would come, one by one by one.

In 2013, her father, David Deal, was given ten years for attempted child abuse. Her aunt, Cynthia Stoltzmann, got twenty-four years behind bars for child abuse. Her grandmother, Judith Deal, was also given ten years for child abuse.

It would be several more years before Ame's killers, Sammantha and John Allen, went on trial for murder.

Sammantha Allen, now 29, was found guilty of first-degree murder on June 26, 2017.

During her trial, jurors learned that before she fell asleep the night Ame died, she debated letting the girl out of her plastic prison.

"I didn't even wake up to go unlock it, and I thought about it," she said.

121

She was sentenced to death on August 7.

Superior Court Judge Teresa Sanders tacked on an additional four consecutive sentences totaling 76 years for four counts of child abuse.

Only one woman has been executed in Arizona: Eva Dugan, who was hanged in 1930 for killing her employer. At her execution, her head was reportedly ripped from her body by the noose, and rolled to the area where spectators were watching, causing some of them to faint from the horror of it all.

Sammantha Allen will go more gently, as Arizona now has implemented lethal injection as its favored method of execution.

Allen's head was down, and her shoulder shook from crying as the verdict was read. It was, jurors said, the first show of emotion they'd seen since proceedings began.

"Lack of remorse was the biggest thing that played into it for us, that we didn't see that from Sammantha throughout the whole process," one juror said outside the courtroom after the sentence was handed down.

John Allen also headed to death row

John Allen, also 29, went on trial October 9, 2017.

During the event, prosecutors told Ame's story, questioning why Allen had hidden the padlock, if the kids were only playing a game.

Jurors learned that John and Sammantha had discussed letting Ame out of the box, but neither felt like going to the garage to do so.

"I just didn't get up," John said.

Salaiz, the first officer on the scene, broke down in tears when he saw the photos of Ame dead on the carpet next to the plastic box that ended up being her coffin.

On November 16, John Allen was also given the death penalty in the death of his wife's young cousin, Ame Deal.

The jury failed to look at Allen when they filed back into court after wrapping up its deliberation as part of the penalty phase of the trial. Allen was convicted of first-degree murder earlier in November.

Maricopa County Superior Court Judge Erin O'Brien Otis sentenced Allen to death by lethal injection, along with 36 years in prison for child abuse and conspiracy to commit child abuse.

"In my entire career, I can't say I've ever seen a worse case," Judge Otis said. "This was one of the most unnecessary deaths of a child I've ever seen."

Unlike his wife, who cried at her sentence, Allen sat motionless before addressing the judge.

"I want to say I'm sorry," he said. "What happened was an accident. I'm an idiot. I'm a jerk. It was an accident. I'm sorry to Ame. I'm sorry to her family. I'm sorry to my family. I shamed all of them."

Shirley Deal, who was not held accountable for abandoning her daughter with people who questioned their family ties with the girl, said that the sentence would never equal the anguish her daughter endured during her short life.

"The death penalty is too good and too easy for you. I want you to suffer till death," Shirley Deal wrote of Ame's tormenters in 2013. "The only thing you deserve is where you are going when you leave this Earth."

For Officer Salaiz, the outcome left more conflicted emotions.

"I'm overjoyed that they were convicted because that's what they deserve for what they did to that little girl. But I'm distraught my testimony puts two people to death," he said. "Do I have sympathy for them? I don't. Because of what they did.

"Here I am, the cop who first arrived on the scene, who knows exactly what happened, who knows they are monsters. I should be doing cartwheels, because not only did they destroy Ame's life and her family's life, they destroyed my life. They made it hell for six years."

Still, he felt a little bit lighter than he had since he walked into the filthy garage where Ame died back in 2011, because his testimony was enough to help put two killers on death row, and enough to allow the officer to put the story away for a while, freeing him from the nightmare of it all.

John and Sammantha Allen are the first husband and wife to be sentenced to death in Arizona.

July

WOMAN KILLED AT TWISTED GENDER REVEAL PARTY

A woman's gender reveal party turned into a nightmare on July 8, when two gunmen flung open the door of the rented wood-frame home and opened fire, killing 22-year-old Autum Garrett of Huntington, Indiana, and injuring eight others, including three children.

A dog was also injured in the shooting, which happened just after 11 p.m., while the 14 houseguests were at home watching a movie.

A gender reveal party usually includes a dramatic moment when either a pregnant woman or her friends and family discover the sex of the baby, often through the cutting of a cake, revealing pink or blue sponge or frosting, or the releasing of pink or blue balloons.

A few hours earlier, Cheyanne Willis had announced on Facebook that her baby was a boy.

In this case, however, the drama came afterwards, when it was revealed that 21-year-old Cheyanne Willis, who told the media that she lost her baby after suffering a gunshot wound to the thigh, was never really pregnant at all.

And police are now full of even more questions about what happened in Colerain Township, Ohio, on that sunny day in July.

Lies stall investigation

The trouble is, the lips of most of those who attended are now pretty much sealed, and what police are getting from witnesses is often less truth than lie, which is making it virtually impossible for police to conduct a successful investigation, according to department spokesman Jim Love.

For the first two weeks of their investigation, police assumed that what they had been told by people who attended the party had been true, and that Willis had really been pregnant with a baby boy. She announced that she lost her baby after she was treated and released from the hospital following her gunshot injury.

According to a post on Facebook, this was allegedly the second time Willis faked a pregnancy.

"We were led to believe an unborn child was murdered in this incident, only to find out that is not the case," police said. "The Colerain Police Department will not comment further on any other misleading information, other than to say we wish our time had been spent on true leads that would help us remove these dangerous criminals from the streets."

Now, they felt frustrated and stonewalled over the uncooperative witnesses in the case.

"All we have at this point is speculation," said Colerain Township police, adding that many man hours have been wasted chasing false leads that were knowingly provided to officers from the first minutes of the investigation.

The public is likely speculating as well, especially given the lies coming from those who attended the party.

Was Willis attempting to cover up a pregnancy lie with an elaborate scheme to open up the opportunity for her to lose her baby?

Did Willis, as some speculated, plan the shooting to set her cousin up due to jealousy over her happy life?

Did the man who thought he was the baby's father decide he wanted out of the situation and planned a hit?

No one knows the real story, but what police know so far is that the shooting was "in no way random," officials said, and they expect multiple arrests after officials finish poring over text messages, emails, and other evidence.

Why did Willis lie?

According to psychologists, women might lie about a pregnancy because it gives them the attention they may crave, either due to narcissism or low self-esteem.

"Some of these young girls are starving for attention no matter if it's positive or negative. Perhaps they see all the attention their peers or siblings got when they were pregnant and crave some of that same attention," says Torey C. Richards, a licensed mental health counselor who has treated girls who have lied about being pregnant. "I often see that their friends, while at times judgmental, often start bonding with the young girl in a nurturing way, something that she doesn't get normally from them."

Mental illness, the desire to reunite with an ex-boyfriend or an overwhelming desire to have a baby (sometimes women lie, then kidnap a newborn to cover their tracks, such as Julia Corey, a Massachusetts woman who in 2009 miscarried, then killed her eight-and-a-half-month pregnant friend and took the baby, pretending it was her own) could also be at the heart of the lie. None, of it, however, will do Willis much good if she ends up being charged with obstructing justice for the impact her lies had on the police investigation into the shooting.

"If you lie to us on the forefront, then it destroys any credibility that you might have as a witness in a court of law," one police officer said.

What happened the day of the party?

At the gender reveal party, Willis had happily announced that her baby was a boy and then quickly posted the good news on Facebook.

A family friend who attended the event, Candice Verga, said that it was a "positive" and "happy" environment at the actual party.

In fact, the day would have been perfect, if someone hadn't started shooting.

After the party was over, several people remained at the home to watch a "Spider-Man" movie. They had just turned out the lights when two gunmen wearing hoodies burst through the front door of the rental property and sprayed the living room with gunfire, firing 14 rounds that left Willis's cousin, Autum Garrett, dead, and Garrett's husband, Bryan, and their two children, a boy, 6, and a girl, 2, among those injured.

Then, it was chaos.

According to Verga, everyone was screaming and crying, trying to make sense of what had just happened in what was later determined to be less than two minutes. Verga scooped up an injured boy and wrapped him in her shirt, then carried him outside to wait for help to arrive.

Four other adults and an eight-year-old child were also injured in the melee.

For Autum's friends and family, the loss was unimaginable.

"It was like a snuff, boom, she's gone," said Garrett's co-worker, Amanda Burns. "It's like you can't believe it."

Garrett, friends said, lived for her family.

She and Bryan were high school sweethearts, married on June 8, 2013, just after graduating from high school.

Their son, Bryan Jr., was born on Christmas Day of that year.

She wrote a love letter of sorts to him on Facebook afterwards.

"I will do anything and everything to make sure you are happy and have an amazing life as a child and on… Your smile makes me feel so good, it lets me know you are happy and that's all I want in life is for you to be happy! You have so much life ahead of you and I'm just going to hold your hand and walk you through life and teach you things, have fun, and love you no matter what you do, because no matter how bad it is I will forgive you before you even ask baby boy, I will bend over backwards for you, I would give my life for you because I just love you that much and I'll do what it takes to protect you!"

She lost that opportunity on that evening in July at a scene that initially left police officers shattered.

Police in the small community were stunned when they arrived at the scene of the shooting, especially after seeing injured children, dressed for bed in their now-bloody pajamas.

"It was horrific, something that was unimaginable," one officer said. "Our hearts are heavy with what we've seen and experienced in our community."

911 was busy that night

At least four people made calls to 911 to report the shooting, which happened at 11:21 p.m. and lasted about two minutes.

"I think a baby's been shot. I think I got hit," one caller said. "There's a whole lot of people here shot. They just ran in and started shooting."

Another person said she was outside in her car when she saw two people, one wearing a blue hoodie, the other in a green hoodie, enter the home. She then heard gunfire and watched the two run out of the home in the working-class neighborhood of Colerain Township.

"There is little kids hurt and everything," she says in the call. "I was sitting in my car, they just ran in and started shooting. There's a pregnant girl here ... Oh, my God."

The woman was unable to establish how many people were injured in the chaos, nor was a neighbor who also made a call.

"Ma'am, all I know is, I don't know what's going on, all I know is she's a neighbor. I was at home minding my business and I just heard someone in distress banging on my door, and a young lady was bleeding and she said she'd been shot and so had someone else and I just tried to come out and see what was going on," said the neighbor.

Police initially said victims were cooperative

Colerain Township Police Chief Mark Denney said at the time that officials were not certain if anyone at the party was specifically targeted or if the fatal gunshots were meant for someone else.

The Cincinnati Police Department was called in to process the crime scene, which included a search of the home after a warrant was issued.

An unloaded gun believed to belong to the renters was found on the lawn, but police said it was not used in the shooting.

Denney said that they had interviewed everyone who was "medically able" to talk about the case and said at the time that witnesses were cooperating with police.

Still, there were many questions that remained unanswered, especially in the early stages of the investigation.

"We are just in the beginning stages of this," Denney said. "There's a lot more questions I can't answer than I can.

"Somebody has information about this," he added. "When three kids get shot, someone has to step forward."

He called on anyone with any knowledge in the case to contact police.

Shooting was likely drug-related

According to police, several of the people attending the party were connected to various local drug circles, making drug-related issues the reason behind the shooting.

It was, police said, "in no way random."

Neighbors were quick to point out that drugs of all kinds were more pervasive these days in their working-class neighborhood.

"There's a lot of drugs in this neighborhood," said Shawn Fee, who said marijuana, opiates and heroin were readily available.

Another neighbor said he'd witnessed several drug deals in the neighborhood.

Notable

According to police, this was not the first act of violence Cheyanne Willis has reported.

In 2014, she said that she'd been a victim of an assault when strangers punched her and wrote on her forehead during an altercation at a local mall.

According to the other woman involved in the fight, Cheyenne Fisher, the meeting that turned messy was just to get her car back.

Fisher had loaned Willis her white Chevy Impala a month earlier in order to get to work, but the arrangement was only temporary, and when she asked for it back, Willis had refused to return the car.

Fisher met with Willis, who brought her ex-boyfriend, on Christmas Eve of 2014 at a local mall parking lot to take back the car.

"We didn't plan on fighting or anything–we just planned on going, getting my car, and leaving," said Fisher, who added that Willis swung first, although that occurred before Willis' ex-boyfriend began taping the exchange.

Willis said she was buying the car from Fisher and had put down an $80 down payment.

In truth, Fisher said, Willis stole the car.

In the video, Fisher and others are shown slapping Willis, slamming her head into the hood of the car, pulling her hair, and pushing her to the ground.

They then wrote "I got my ass whooped" on Willis' forehead in black eyeliner, signing their names to their handiwork.

Willis said she got a concussion in the attack.

Ultimately, no charges were filed.

One theory could make sense

While many are speculating over what really happened in the gender reveal party, one theory from a reader commenting on an online Fox News story regarding the shooting does seem plausible.

The reader suggests that Willis herself set up the shooting, allegedly carried out by her boyfriend and another friend. The instigators meant to injure people at the party, especially children, creating an opportunity for them to then raise money on GoFundMe.

"She and some of the participants in this party who gave lying stories to the cops to get them off the scent of the shooters were in on a grift, a plan to set up a GoFundMe page after this story of a mass shooting in women and children's legs went national," wrote one person on Facebook. "They would have divvied up the money with the shooters. But someone died, and that scared them into trying to protect their skins. How do grifts work? You take advantage of the innocence of strangers. This is a piece of work who is guilty of murder if the cops can start interrogating the liars here. They hoped for big bucks on the emotional appeal of this story, but the lies have started to come untangled."

FOUR MEN GO MISSING IN PENNSYLVANIA UNDER MYSTERIOUS CIRCUMSTANCES

When 20-year-old Cosmo DiNardo of Bucks County, Pennsylvania, tried to sell 21-year-old Tom Meo's 1996 Nissan Maxima for $500, Meo's diabetic testing kit and his supplies were still in the vehicle.

The man who had been reported missing by his family a day earlier never went anywhere without those things. For a Type 1 diabetic, it would have been foolhardy at best to leave it behind.

When police found out, they were immediately suspicious. His family and friends were frantic.

Meo, from Plumstead Township, had not been seen since Friday, when his girlfriend said he'd gone missing. His family reported their son's disappearance the next day.

Meo, however, was not the only young man missing in Bucks County.

Also missing were 19-year-old Dean A. Finocchiaro of Middletown Township, 22-year-old Mark P. Sturgis of Pennsburg, a community in nearby Montgomery County, and 19-year-old Jimi T. Patrick of Newtown Township.

Patrick had been reported missing by his grandfather on July 6, when he failed to show up for work that day.

Both Meo and Sturgis–best friends who worked together at a construction company owned by Sturgis' father, Mark Potash–failed to show up for work on July 8.

"I thought maybe they had a night of drinking and slept somewhere," Potash said. "That was my hope."

DiNardo, who grew up and still lived in the middle-class suburb of

Bensalem, was the oldest child of local business owners Antonio and Sandra DiNardo. Antonio, who went by Tony, owned a concrete company, Metro Ready Mix and Supply, as well as a real estate portfolio he'd inherited after the death of his father, after whom Cosmo DiNardo was named. Sandra DiNardo ran a trucking company, Bella Trucking.

A familiar face in the neighborhood, Cosmo DiNardo was thought to be friendly with all four men, and when another friend messaged him on Facebook about one of the missing men, Dean Finocchiaro, (perhaps tellingly referring to him as "deadman, I mean Deanman"), DiNardo's reply was emotionless, aside from the attempt to throw anyone who was suspicious off his trail.

"I mean I know the kid but, yeah, I feel bad for his parents. He's a pill-popping junky who had 2 duis (sic) and got popped for stolen bikes and guns He prob just jumped parole Or probation," DiNardo quickly wrote.

Of course, DiNardo knew where Finocchiaro was, and he had not jumped parole.

According to reports, Finocchiaro had been last seen being picked up at his home by DiNardo, who told police during initial questioning that he had driven Finocchiaro around until the other man told him he was on his way to "do a big coke deal," DiNardo said, adding that at that point, he kicked the man out of his truck and went fishing.

There was an attempted drug deal, as it happened. But DiNardo did not kick Finocchiaro out of his truck, and he did not go fishing.

Suspicion mounts for DiNardo

Early on July 9, police found Sturgis' unoccupied car at a local market. Less than two miles away was Meo's car, including his diabetes supplies that he needed to survive.

Police immediately focused on the DiNardo property in Solebury Township, a remote 90-acre property that was unoccupied but included outbuildings and heavy equipment, and descended on the vast expanse of land with police dogs, officers, and a helicopter.

Based on the terrain, which would make finding the missing men akin to the proverbial needle in a haystack, police made an appeal to the public and arrested DiNardo on a prior gun charge that had been dropped, and persuaded a judge to set bail at $1 million, calling DiNardo a "person of interest" in the disappearance of the missing men.

Police then got to work and "worked tirelessly, selflessly, nonstop around the clock, in the sweltering heat and the dust and the pouring-down rain," Bucks County District Attorney Matthew D. Weintraub said.

"We have recovered several important pieces of evidence at this site that we're currently working very hard on with the majority of our manpower and at other locations," Weintraub told reporters who were gathered at the scene. "This is just really, really rough on everybody involved because of the heat, the magnitude, the scope and the stakes are incredibly high–life and death."

After learning that their missing loved ones were likely on the DiNardo property, many family members of the four men spent hours baking under a hot summer sun as investigators sifted through the desecrated remains.

"Simply losing a loved one is overwhelming," said Bucks County assistant DA Gregg Shore. "What they've had to do, sitting through 96 painstaking hours at a site where weather conditions were awful at times, to see whether their loved ones are in the ground, that has been an overwhelming experience for them."

As police searched, DiNardo posted bail with a $100,000 cashier's check from his father, Antonio, and left Bensalem Jail & Prison.

After a witness said DiNardo had attempted to sell him Meo's Nissan for $500, police rearrested DiNardo within 24 hours, charging him with possession of stolen property.

This time, officials set his bond at $5 million, and said that DiNardo's history of mental illness—he had been diagnosed with schizophrenia—made him too much of a flight risk, especially so given his links to at least one of the other missing men, as well as a previous arrest for gun possession despite his having been involuntarily committed for his mental health issues. His mother, Sandra DiNardo, signed the paperwork in July of 2016. Around the same time, he suffered a head injury while riding his ATV, which some people attributed to his increasingly erratic behavior.

"That incident drove him over the edge. He was a more violent individual," said a friend regarding the ATV accident, which left DiNardo with broken bones in addition to the head injury.

The news that he was the last one to be seen with Finocchiaro put DiNardo under more scrutiny.

The bail was so high because the prosecutor believed DiNardo, who had access to plenty of money from his family's lucrative real estate and construction business, was "even more of a flight risk at this point."

Search for missing men continues

With DiNardo at least temporarily behind bars, police stepped up their search for the missing men, using the car in DiNardo's possession as a piece of the puzzle.

Ultimately, it was signals from one of the men's cell phones as well as an assist from cadaver dogs, that found a mass grave containing three of the men, their bodies doused with gasoline and set ablaze.

"This was a homicide. Make no doubt about it," said Weintraub during a news conference after the discovery of the mass grave. "I don't understand the science behind it, but those dogs could smell these poor boys 12 ½ feet below the ground."

After the bodies were found, there was a discussion at the jail, and DiNardo confessed to killing the four missing men, implicating his cousin, 20-year-old Sean Kratz, in the crimes.

DiNardo and Kratz had only recently connected, and the first murder was the first time Kratz had been to his cousin's family property.

Because police had only found three of the bodies, in exchange for information about where the fourth man was buried, the DA took the death penalty off the table.

Patrick was buried almost a half-mile from the mass grave, and police would likely not have found it without help from DiNardo.

"It was so far away that I started getting sick to my stomach on the ride," Weintraub said.

Cousins were monsters, confessions reveal

Patrick, who was a year behind DiNardo at Holy Ghost Preparatory School, the Catholic high school the two had both attended and where Patrick was a standout baseball player, was the first to die, on July 5.

According to DiNardo's confession, the two had met up after DiNardo agreed to sell the other man four pounds of marijuana for $8,000.

Patrick, a business major, had just wrapped up his freshman year by making the dean's list at Maryland's Loyola University, which he was attending on a full scholarship.

He was spending the summer working at a Buckingham restaurant. Friends described him as "such a people person."

But, DiNardo said, when he picked Patrick up, he had only brought

$800 with him, which enraged the volatile DiNardo. DiNardo responded by taking his former classmate to a remote part of the family's acreage, where he shot him with a .22-caliber rifle before digging a six-foot ditch with a backhoe and burying him there.

Apparently, that first blood was exhilarating for DiNardo, who choose Finocchiaro as his next victim.

He set up a meeting for July 7 on the pretense of a drug deal and picked up his cousin, 20-year-old Sean Kratz, on the way. As they headed for the meeting at the DiNardo property, the two hatched a plan to rob Finocchiaro.

Once Finocchiaro arrived, the cousins drove him to a barn on the property on an ATV, where Finocchiaro was shot in the head. (Both DiNardo and Kratz blamed their cousin for the murder.)

Kratz later told police that he threw up immediately after the shooting.

DiNardo wrapped Finocchiaro's body in a blue tarp and attempted to drag the body from the barn, but the tarp got stuck on a nail.

He then moved the body with the backhoe, dumping it into a converted oil tank that DiNardo referred to as "a pig roaster."

The two then prepared for another drug deal that DiNardo had set up for the evening.

DiNardo originally met his prospective buyers–Meo and Sturgis–in a church parking lot, then asked the two men to follow him back to the family property, where Kratz was waiting.

It did not take long for DiNardo's bloodlust to kick in.

"When they turned their backs on me, I shot Tom in the back," DiNardo told investigators.

As Meo fell to the ground, screaming, Sturgis attempted to flee, but DiNardo shot him too, killing him with a single bullet from a .357

Smith & Wesson handgun owned by his mother, then, out of ammunition, used a backhoe to crush Meo, finally putting him out of his misery and silencing the screams. He used the backhoe to dump the two new bodies in the metal tank where Finocchiaro was stashed. He and his cousin then poured gasoline over the corpses and lit them on fire.

The cousins then went for a late dinner at Steve's Prince of Steaks in Northern Philadelphia before heading to DiNardo's place in Bensalem, where Kratz spent the night.

The next day, the two returned to bury the converted oil tank 12 ½ feet beneath the ground.

After the first three bodies–those of Finocchiaro, Meo and Sturgis– were found burned in the oil drum in a deep mass grave on the family's 90-acre property, DiNardo led investigators to the fourth victim, Patrick, who was buried in a separate location.

On the night he was arrested, police interrogated Kratz in an effort to determine where the murder weapons were hidden. Although he initially denied any knowledge of the weapons, eventually he and his mother led police to Kratz's aunt's property, where he had hidden the weapons.

Ironically for DiNardo, who had been appointed to a drug and alcohol committee, each death was tied to a drug deal reportedly gone bad, if DiNardo's version of events is true.

"Every death was related to a purported drug transaction, and at the end of each one there's a killing," said one insider close to the story.

Later, District Judge Maggie Snow ordered DiNardo–who attended his arraignment hearing from his jail cell via video wearing an orange jumpsuit and glasses–held without bond until the preliminary hearing.

Both DiNardo and Kratz are charged with homicide, conspiracy,

139

abuse of corpses, and other crimes. DiNardo faces a mandatory sentence of life in prison if convicted.

"He's accused of committing four homicides in one week," Snow said. "He's a tremendous danger to the community."

DiNardo apologized to police when he confessed to the crimes. The confession was in exchange for the district attorney to take the death penalty off the table.

"I can tell you, for I've been there, we'd still be looking for Jimi Patrick had we not made this agreement," Weintraub said, adding that the burial site was not close to the mass grave housing the other three victims.

"I am very, very relieved to say that we brought four young men one step closer to their loved ones," he added. "Our boys get to go home to their families, which was always our priority."

For the families of those killed, it was little consolation.

"The Finocchiaros have been doing terribly," their lawyer, Thomas R. Kline, said. "All inexplicable, all tragic, all unnecessary. They're committed to seeing that Mr. DiNardo spends the rest of his life in jail."

DiNardo had an uber-bright future

By all accounts, DiNardo had a charmed life. He was heir to the sizeable real estate and construction fortune owned by his parents in the suburbs of Philadelphia, about 45 miles away from the family's 90-acre estate where he and his cousin executed the four men.

Although other members said he rarely attended the once-monthly meetings, DiNardo had been appointed by the mayor to the Bensalem Township's Drug and Alcohol Advisory Board in both 2015 and 2016.

But he always was a bit of a bully, despite the fortune he was set to inherit, or perhaps as a sense of entitlement because of it.

He stalked girls until they blocked him on social media, and he was banned from both his high school campus as well as the campus of the university he had attended after he dropped out because he returned to harass other people.

His social media feeds were equally telling. One Facebook post included a photo of him, shirtless and pointing a revolver.

It was chilling stuff for someone who had so much going for him, but like the subject of "The Making of a Murderer," Steven Avery, who was set to win millions in a lawsuit against Manitowoc County, Wisconsin, after spending more than a decade in prison for a sexual assault he didn't commit, some people don't know how good they've got it. DiNardo was apparently one of them.

He had already bragged to friends about seeing people killed, or killing people in Philly, depending on whom you asked.

"He's told me and my friends, 'Yeah, I've killed people before, I just haven't been caught,'" said one acquaintance. "We literally were just like, 'Yeah, all right, Cosmo, sure you did.'"

Those who knew DiNardo said that after a 2016 ATV accident, all of the unsavory qualities DiNardo had previously exhibited came on even stronger.

His mood turned dark, and his personality changed enough that he drove away even his closest friends.

Chris Hellmuth had been DiNardo's friend since fourth grade, but after the accident, when DiNardo had a brief hospital stay for mental health issues, they grew apart.

Still, it was hard for Hellmuth to see his old friend as a mass murderer.

"The Cosmo I knew for over 10 years would never be capable of anything like this," he wrote on DiNardo's Facebook page.

But others saw things differently and considered the boy who could bench press 220 pounds by eighth grade to be a serious threat.

"Cosmo was crazy," said Amber Peters, 20, whose boyfriend was once one of DiNardo's closer friends. "He's been talking about killing people since he was 14."

At 15, Cosmo punched two guys he didn't know when he saw them talking to his girlfriend, and he also bragged that the same year, he'd killed two people in Philadelphia. (After his arrest, he also told police that he had killed two people in Philadelphia, which if proven to be true, would erase his confession deal and put the death penalty back on the table.)

As for why DiNardo choose to kill four men so callously, there are no good answers.

"I don't know that," Weintraub said. "I'm not really sure we could ever answer that question."

BOYFRIEND OF MISSING WOMAN HID CORPSE IN FREEZER AS NEW GIRLFRIEND MOVED IN

For one Ohio man, breaking up was hard to do, especially so around Valentine's Day.

Holidays, experts say, are the worst times to end a relationship, because significant dates on a calendar like the holiday of love can lead to so much stress.

"Everything about the holidays reminds us of family, love and ritual," Kathleen Hall, CEO of Atlanta's Stress Institute, told Match.com. "We see emotional movies. We go to the mall and see lovers holding hands. We go to restaurants and see couples kissing and eating together. Holidays are a sensual time of smells, food, music, lights, and decorations. It is a time that we naturally want to share with another person."

Splitting up would bring on so much anxiety, right? Especially if you've already got someone you like a whole lot more than your current partner.

Apparently, that's what drove 31-year-old Arturo Novoa to skip the breakup talk and go straight to murder.

Instead of sitting down and having a sad Valentine's Day talk with his girlfriend, 28-year-old Shannon Graves, police believe Novoa killed her, allegedly dismembering her body and putting it on ice.

Within a few months, Graves had moved a new girlfriend, 34-year-old Katrina Layton, in.

She, apparently, was aware of Graves' death, because she had no trouble using all of the dead woman's things, which were still filling at least half of Novoa's apartment.

"Basically, Miss Layton moved in with Mr. Novoa and started living her life," Youngstown Prosecutor Dana Lantz said at a news conference. "She didn't hold herself out to be Shannon. She just lived her life, using her phone, caring for her dog."

Novoa tells family Graves ditched him for another guy

At first, Shannon Graves' loved ones weren't too concerned that she was missing. Apparently, she was struggling with addiction and often went off the grid, sometimes disappearing for months at a time.

But when friends and family members attempted to contact her, Novoa's response made it all seem a little bit fishy.

He allegedly told her family and friends that she'd left him for another man, but they thought there might be more to the story when they didn't hear from Graves either at Easter or during her sister's birthday.

Even though she struggled with drugs, she had never missed the family's special events, they said.

Plus, she had recently graduated from Raphael's School of Beauty in Boardman and was planning to begin a new career in the beauty industry.

Graves was reported missing in June, but the family said she was last seen in Youngstown, Ohio, in February, when a sister saw her with Novoa.

It is not certain when Novoa killed her and stashed her in the freezer, although that time frame seems likely.

Landlady gets a gruesome surprise

At some point, however, probably around the time her family reported her missing, Novoa decided he needed to find new digs for Graves' body.

To erase at least some of the evidence connecting him with his former girlfriend, he turned to his landlord of four years, Ken Easenbaugh, for help with his problem.

According to The New York Post, "Novoa had asked his landlord if he could move an upright freezer down to the landlord's basement because his electricity had been shut off, and 'he didn't want his freezer full of meat to spoil.'"

Unfortunately for Novoa, he didn't count on his landlord's nosy, hungry wife.

She grew suspicious when she noticed a padlock had been placed on the freezer, and she couldn't contain her curiosity about the appliance's contents given that ominous padlock.

On July 30, almost a month after Novoa asked them to store the freezer, the wife got her chance to inspect the inside of the appliance. When a plan to make spaghetti and meatballs was thwarted by a lack of ground beef in her own freezer, she decided to check out Novoa's meat-filled freezer to borrow some of his.

"She thought she would borrow some hamburger from the freezer and simply replace it later," her husband said.

She pried off the padlock and successfully opened the door, but when she saw a large garbage bag in the freezer instead of packages of meat, she got "a bad feeling," shut the freezer door and waited for her husband to come home, Easenbaugh said.

When he did arrive home, he sliced open the bag, only to find a frozen human foot.

Other bags also contained body parts.

Meanwhile, over at Novoa's place...

Layton had moved into Novoa's apartment in June, according to the New York Post, but unlike most moves, hers wasn't too stressful.

She already had at her disposal a telephone, a car, credit cards, and a dog, all courtesy of her boyfriend's missing girlfriend.

And Novoa, well, he had a criminal history.

A felon, Novoa had spent time in the state penitentiary and then was convicted for having a gun, which was illegal due to his prior felony conviction.

His charges also included a 2006 incident involving aggravated arson and obstructing official business after he threw a flaming object onto the porch of a home on Cooper Street, where Novoa himself lived. Easenbaugh apparently didn't do much of a background check before letting Novoa move in.

In 2010, Novoa was indicted by a Mahoning County grand jury on charges of illegal gun possession, and in 2015, he was arrested for possession of marijuana.

At the time of his most recent arrest, Novoa was working in the kitchen of a restaurant in Boardman, a suburb of Youngstown.

He was also living under an assumed name. As far as his landlord and employer were concerned, Novoa was Anthony Gonzales, likely in an attempt to disguise his record.

Both Novoa and Layton were arrested and jailed on charges of corpse abuse under a $1 million bond.

Layton told police she bought the freezer for Novoa in early July and also supplied Novoa with an extension cord.

"No one was charged with a murder because we have no idea what the cause of death was," Youngstown Police Lieutenant Doug Bobovnik said.

Family remembers dead woman

Several months after Novoa and Layton were arrested, Graves' family held a memorial at a local park, all coming together for an evening to remember a woman they loved for the unique way she looked at the world.

"Shannon was a free spirit," said her sister, Debbie DePaul, who rescued her sister's dog, Molly, from the apartment she had once shared with Novoa.

And even though they often went months without seeing her, knowing that they never will see her again has been trying for the family.

"It's not the easiest," Debbie said. "I have my moments, but I'm just trying to stay strong and keep going."

It's been especially important for Debbie to stay strong for their father, Ronnie De Paul, who was pleased with the number of people who showed up to honor his daughter's memory.

Still, her murder is beyond his comprehension, and seeing so many loved ones coming to pay tribute to his daughter is only accentuating his pain.

"What I don't understand is what she could have done to have these two people to do what they did to her," Ronnie De Paul said. "I only got to bury part of a body."

One of those friends was John Skarada, who had an idea something wasn't right as soon as they realized Shannon was missing.

"I knew it before I heard it," Skarada said. "Just everything around her being missing wasn't right. We kind of didn't know the specifics or gruesomeness of it, but figured pretty much something like that had happened."

Despite the horror of how she died, Skarada chose to remember Shannon at her best.

"She was awesome, always full of energy. She was a great person," Skarada said.

That was how he will think of her from now on. The foul nature of her death won't be included in his memories.

August

HEATHER HEYER DIED
FIGHTING AGAINST HATE

On August 12, 32-year-old paralegal Heather D. Heyer joined a group of counter-protesters at the University of Virginia Charlottesville to stand against a rally by alt-right protesters who'd gathered to protect a statue of Confederate general Robert E. Lee, which was slated for removal from the city's Emancipation Park.

The Unite the Right rally had been organized by Vanguard America, a hate group that appropriated the Nazi slogan "blood and soil" as its own, and had drawn support from neo-Nazis, factions of the Ku Klux Klan, and skinheads.

It was planned, according to the group's Facebook page, to "affirm the rights of Southerners and white people to organize for their interests."

One of the group's organizers was former Ku Klux Klan Imperial Wizard David Duke, who told a reporter, "We are going to fulfill the promises of Donald Trump. That's why we voted for Donald Trump, because he said he's going to take our country back."

Heyer had been worried about the possibility of violence, friends said, but she felt it was important to speak out against injustices.

"If you knew Heather, you would know that she loves everyone, and all she wants is equality for everyone, no matter who you love, no matter what color you are," said Heyer's friend and co-worker Marissa Blair, who attended the rally with Heyer.

Heyer died standing up for those beliefs, when a member of the alt-right, James Alex Fields Jr., 20, of Maumee, Ohio, plowed his silver Dodge Challenger with tinted windows into a group of counter-protesters that included Heyer, then drove away.

"She was always passionate about the beliefs she held," her father, Mark Heyer, said in an interview with CNN. "She had a bigger backbone than I did."

Ultimately, it made her a martyr, because she died standing up for those beliefs.

"She was very strong in what she felt, and she spoke with conviction," Blair added. "She would never back down from what she believed in. And that's what she died doing, she died fighting for what she believed in. We didn't want neo-Nazis and alt-right and racists to come into our city and think they could spread freely their hate and their bigotry and their racism. We wanted to let them know that we were about love, that we were overpower them. We were peacefully protesting, and we were just standing up for what we believe in."

Before the hit-and-run, fights had broken out between the alt-right group and counter-protestors. Police had broken up the rally and protesters and counter-protesters were beginning to disperse when Fields drove his vehicle into the crowd, striking and killing Heyer and injuring 34 others.

According to Blair, the accident happened in seconds, and before he had a chance to assess what had happened, bodies were flying along the sidewalk and the street where they had just been marching.

Rally had kicked off under the cover of darkness

Protests had begun the night before, when alt-right members from various groups nationwide descended on the University of Virginia campus wielding Tiki torches and marching two by two, chanting their hate-filled slogans, "Blood and soil," "You will not replace us" and "Jews will not replace us."

Many were dressed as Hitler's child soldiers, Hitler's Youth, wearing shorts and the WWII haircut favored by the Führer himself, with side-swept bangs and sharply shorn sides.

The infantilism of the men, most of them young, in their early 20s, was oddly juxtaposed against a hate-fueled mission to bring validity to beliefs that have been festering since the Civil Rights era, but have recently crept out of the shadows by an alt-right made more emboldened by the uncensored U.S. president who counts them among his supporters.

These men, no matter how innocently they were dressed, were not coming in peace. And when they reached the campus's statue of Thomas Jefferson, they were met by 30 University of Virginia students, who had locked arms and were surrounding the statue.

Almost immediately, there was chaos.

Both sides sprayed pepper spray and threw punches. The alt-right protesters escalated the violence by throwing their flaming torches at the students.

Initially, only one campus police officer was on hand to quell the violence, and it was several minutes before law enforcement reinforcements showed up.

Both sides suffered injuries, and one witness reported seeing a woman in a wheelchair being doused with lighter fluid by one of the alt-right protestors just before police broke up the gathering.

Second day of confrontation begins

The next day, the alt-right rally was scheduled to run from noon to 5 p.m., but by 8 a.m., people were already filling the park, including a group of clergy members who sang "This Little Light of Mine" while white nationalists shouted, "Our blood, our soil."

Virginia Governor Terry McAuliffe declared a state of emergency in anticipation of violence.

A militia group also showed up, brandishing weapons in the open-carry state, and said they were there to help maintain peace between the two sides.

"The militia showed up with long rifles, and we were concerned to have that in the mix," Virginia Secretary of Public Safety and Homeland Security Brian Moran told the Washington Post. "They seemed like they weren't there to cause trouble, but it was a concern to have rifles in that kind of environment."

Both Virginia State Police and Charlottesville police officers were stationed at the park, but they were only at the back of the park and along the sides. There were no officers covering the front of the park, where tensions quickly escalated.

By 11 a.m., white nationalists armed with clubs and shields, and counter-protesters carrying sticks and balloons, filled with paint and ink were battling violently with no police intervention.

According to Moran, the delay was because officers had to quickly make a change from their regular uniforms into armor, which would better protect them as they waded into the fray.

But when rocks and bottles began flying between the two factions, police stepped in and at 11:22 a.m., declared an unlawful assembly.

They thought the disturbance had been put to rest.

The worst is yet to come

The crowd began to slowly disperse, about four hours before the rally–for which organizers had secured a permit–had been scheduled to end.

Police and nearby residents likely breathed a sigh of relief as they watched the club-wielding white supremacists and those protesting their presence at the park leave.

That relief, however, would be short-lived.

At 1:14 p.m., there was a tweet from Charlottesville's city Twitter account that didn't seem connected to the rally: "CPD & VSP respond to 3-vehicle crash at Water & 4th Streets. Several pedestrians struck. Multiple injuries."

Those at the scene, however, immediately knew that there was a clear link between the crash and the rally.

Matthew Korbon was standing on the sidewalk when Fields, who earlier in the day had been photographed carrying a shield affiliated with the group Vanguard America, allegedly drove his Challenger into the group of counter-protesters who were leaving the park.

It was "absolutely intentional," said Korbon, who said he watched Fields drive directly into one group of pedestrians who were walking away and had their backs to the vehicle before putting his car into reverse and backing into another group.

"I saw what I thought was an explosion out of the corner of my eye," said Adam Senecaut of De Moines, who was among the counter-protestors. "But it was really bodies flying. I was prepared for some type of violence, but the kind of terror we saw was unlike anything I've ever seen."

People flew into the air "like they were just bowling pins. It was just terrifying," 23-year-old Thomas Pilnik told HuffPost.

Other witnesses told the same story.

"I was standing on the edge of the crowd and I saw the bodies fly," Kristen Leigh told the New York Daily News. "There was a car pummeling through us ... bodies flying through the air."

When the dust settled, Heather Heyer was dead, a victim of blunt force trauma to the chest, according to the results of an autopsy that were released in October.

Later that day, two Virginia State troopers were killed when their helicopter crashed in a wooded area on the outskirts of Charlottesville.

According to Virginia State Police, the helicopter was assisting law enforcement officers on the ground when it went down.

Lt. H. Jay Cullen, 48, of Midlothian, Va., and trooper pilot Berke M.M. Bates, 40, of Quinton, Va., were killed in the crash, which occurred in a wooded residential area outside of Charlottesville at about 5 p.m.

Charlottesville Mayor Mike Signer directed much of the blame toward a divisive political climate that at the time of the incident included white supremacist and executive chairman of the alt-right website Breitbart News Steve Bannon in a place of power as Chief Strategist of the Trump administration.

"I'm not going to make any bones about it. I place the blame for a lot of what you're seeing in America right at the doorstep of the White House and the people around the president," Signer said.

Gov. Terry McAuliffe also made clear his feelings about the divisiveness taking over his state.

"Go home," he said as part of a press conference. "You are not wanted in this great commonwealth. Shame on you. You pretend that you are patriots, but you are anything but a patriot."

Heyer remembered in a televised ceremony

"They tried to kill my child to shut her up, but guess what, you just magnified her," said Heyer's mother, Susan Bro, who spoke in front of a full house at the Charlottesville theater where Heyer's memorial service was held four days after her death.

The event was streamed live on social media.

She made a plea to those in attendance to continue the path that Heyer had forged by continuing to speak out against the hatred and bigotry that ultimately led to her death.

"I want this to spread," said Bro. "I'd rather have my child, but by golly if I got to give her up, we're going to make it count. This is just the beginning of Heather's legacy."

Virginia Governor Terry McAuliffe and Virginia Senator (and vice-presidential candidate on the Democratic ticket with Hillary Clinton) Tim Kaine were among those in attendance.

The memorial was peaceful and included a woman who played "Amazing Grace" and "America the Beautiful" on the saxophone.

Through tears, Heyer's father, Mark Heyer, remembered his daughter's strong convictions.

"She loved people; she wanted equality," he said. "On the day of her passing, she wanted to put down hate."

Heyer's former boss also praised the late paralegal for her determination to protect others from discrimination, which led her down the career path she ultimately chose.

"Heather was a very strong woman," said Alfred A. Wilson, manager of the bankruptcy division at the Miller Law Group in Charlottesville, where she worked as a paralegal. She stood up against "any type of discrimination. That's just how she's always been."

He told the room of more than 1,000 people that Heyer ended a romance when her date questioned her friendship with her African-American boss.

"Maybe if you didn't speak so loudly, they wouldn't have heard you, and you would still be here," said another co-worker, Feda Khateeb-Wilson. "But thank you for making the word 'hate' real... Thank you for making the word 'love' even stronger."

There were no reports of problems around the theater.

A candlelight vigil for Heyer, who in addition to her family, was survived by her Chihuahua, Violet, followed the service.

Incident sparks political travesty

On August 15, the day before Heather Heyer's memorial service, during a press conference once meant to discuss the nation's infrastructure, President Donald Trump soon went off the rails when questioned about his slow response to the deadly incident that resulted in Heyer's death.

Before the night was over, late-night pundits–and the Twittersphere Trump favors–were deriding and ridiculing his support of the white supremacist faction.

"As I said, remember, Saturday, we condemn in the strongest possible terms this egregious display of hatred, bigotry and violence. It has no place in America. And then I went on from there. Here is the thing. Excuse me. Take it nice and easy. Here is the thing. When I make a statement, I like to be correct... and unlike the media, before I make a statement, I like to know the facts.

"What about the alt-left that came charging at—Excuse me—What about the alt-left that came charging at the, as you say, the alt-right? Do they have any semblance of guilt? Let me ask you this: What about the fact that they came charging, that they came charging with clubs in their hands swinging clubs? Do they have any problem? I think they do. So, you know, as far as I'm concerned, that was a horrible, horrible day.

"Wait a minute. I'm not finished. I'm not finished, fake news. That was a horrible day. I will tell you something. I watched those very closely, much more closely than you people watched it. And you had a group on one side that was bad, and you had a group on the other side that was also very violent. And nobody wants to say that. But

I'll say it right now.

"You had a group on the other side that came charging in without a permit and they were very, very violent. All of those people — Excuse me — I've condemned neo-Nazis. I've condemned many different groups. But not all of those people were neo-Nazis, believe me. Not all of those people were white supremacists by any stretch. Those people were also there because they wanted to protest the taking down of a statue, Robert E. Lee.

"I am not putting anybody on a moral plane. What I'm saying is this: You had a group on one side and you had a group on the other and they came at each other with clubs and it was vicious and horrible. And it was a horrible thing to watch. But there is another side. There was a group on this side, you can call them the left. You have just called them the left, that came violently attacking the other group. So, you can say what you want, but that's the way it is... I think there is blame on both sides. You look at both sides. I think there is blame on both sides... You had some very bad people in that group. But you also had people that were very fine people on both sides. You had many people in that group other than neo-Nazis and white nationalists. O.K.? And the press has treated them absolutely unfairly.

"Now, in the other group also, you had some fine people, but you also had troublemakers and you see them come with the black outfits and with the helmets and with the baseball bats. You had a lot of bad people in the other group too.

"There were people in that rally... they were people protesting very quietly the taking down the statue of Robert E. Lee. I am sure in that group there were some bad ones. The following day, it looked like they had some rough, bad people, neo-Nazis, white nationalists, whatever you want to call them. But you had a lot of people in that group that were there to innocently protest and very legally protest.

Because I don't know if you know, they had a permit. The other group didn't have a permit. So, I only tell you this. There are two sides to a story. I thought what took place was a horrible moment for our country, a horrible moment. But there are two sides to the country."

With his statement, Trump clearly defined those sides, according to political pundits who said the incident placed a schism in an already divided nation.

Politicians, both Democratic and Republican, condemned the president's statements.

"We should call evil by its name," said Senator Orrin Hatch of Utah. "My brother didn't give his life fighting Hitler for Nazi ideas to go unchallenged here at home."

A look at the Nazi sympathizer who sparked national conversation

Fields was described by former classmates and teachers as a Nazi sympathizer.

Derek Weimer, a social studies teacher at Randall K. Cooper High School, which Fields attended, said he recognized that Fields had extremist views fueled by a degree of rage caused by his feelings of oppression or persecution.

"He really bought into this white supremacist thing. He was very big into Nazism. He really had a fondness for Adolf Hitler," said Weimer, who said that he and other teachers attempted to use history to change Fields' point of view, only to have his efforts fall on deaf ears.

In August of 2015, Fields entered the U.S. Army but left in December of that year for failing to meet training standards.

Following the death of Heather Heyer, Fields was charged with second-degree murder, five counts of malicious wounding, three counts of aggravated malicious wounding and one count of hit-and-run.

He is currently being housed at the Albemarle-Charlottesville Regional Jail.

The aftermath

In October, white nationalist Richard Spencer told students at the University of Florida in Gainesville that Fields was "attacked" when he drove into the crowd of counter-protesters in Charlottesville, killing Heather Heyer.

Fields, Spencer said, was "used as a scapegoat. His vehicle was attacked" and he was attempting to escape, despite witnesses who have said that Fields drove very deliberately into a group of people walking away, the equivalent of shooting someone in the back.

"What happened with the death of Heather Heyer remains unclear," he added.

September

COLD MEDICINE MADE HIM DO IT

A man who said he'd taken too much cold medicine stabbed his wife 123 times, allegedly in his Coricidin-induced sleep.

In the early hours of September 1, a 28-year-old Raleigh, North Carolina, told a 911 operator that he woke from putting himself to sleep with cold medicine to find his wife of less than a year stabbed to death and himself drenched in her blood.

Matthew Phelps, 28, told the 911 dispatcher that he may have accidentally killed his wife in his sleep.

"I think I killed my wife," Phelps said to the operator, who responded, "What do you mean by that? What happened?"

"I had a dream and then I turned on the lights and she's dead on the floor ... I have blood all over me and there's a bloody knife on the bed. I think I did it. I can't believe this," Phelps continued.

His wife, 29-year-old Lauren Ashley-Nicole Hugelmaier Phelps, was dead from multiple stab wounds, the iron scent of her blood likely filling the room.

According to Phelps Facebook page, he was studying to be a pastor at the time of his wife's murder.

"She's not moving at all," Phelps told the dispatcher, growing increasingly agitated as he paced the room. "Oh, my God. She didn't deserve this."

During the seven-minute call, Phelps said he'd taken Coricidin Cough & Cold because he often had trouble with insomnia.

"I know it can make you feel good," he said. "A lot of times I can't sleep at night. I took more medicine than I should have."

According to Bayer, the makers of Coricidin, there is no relationship between the Cough & Cold formula, specifically formulated to not elevate blood pressure, and savage, aggressive acts, although two of the medicine's ingredients, dextromethorphan and chlorpheniramine, have been linked to psychoses when taken in high doses, which is typically a result of recreational use.

(One of the most memorable scenes in "The Basketball Diaries," a movie based on New York City-born author and musician Jim Carroll's heroin addiction starring Leonardo DiCaprio features the character downing a whole bottle of cough syrup in an effort to get high.)

The dispatcher asked if Phelps' wife could be assisted, and he said, "I don't know. I'm too scared to get too close to her. ... I'm so scared."

Defense not uncommon, but other signs were there

According to Brad Garrett, a former FBI agent, Phelps' cough medicine defense is not as much of a stretch as it might initially appear.

"He qualifies that, yes it does look like I did kill her," Garrett said. "'The knife is here. I have blood all over me. However, this medicine made me do it.' That's not an uncommon way for people in his position to respond."

According to friends, Matthew Phelps had been experiencing dark moods lately, according to posts on his Instagram account, but the murder of his wife was still a shock to those who knew him.

"I saw them come and go, but never a hint of any problems," said neighbor Steve Whitaker, a former president of the homeowner's association of the community where the couple lived. "It's a shock, a young woman losing her life like that."

Phelps was charged with first-degree murder shortly after making the 911 call.

According to an autopsy, Lauren Ashley-Nicole Hugelmaier Phelps sustained twenty-four stab wounds and twenty cuts to her head and neck, thirteen stab wounds and eleven cuts to her torso, sixteen cuts and one stab wound on her right arm and thirty-five cuts and three stab wounds to her left arm.

His defense attorney, Joe Cheshire, said if a jury believes Phelps was under the influence of medication, his charges could be reduced to second-degree murder.

That would take the possibility of the death penalty off the table.

Lauren Ashley-Nicole Hugelmaier Phelps was born in Los Angeles and graduated from Appalachian State University in North Carolina in 2011 with a degree in business administration and management. She worked as an auditor and operated a personal sales business, according to her family.

Is sleep killing a plausible defense?

In 1987, 23-year-old Toronto man Kenneth Parks had a gambling problem that led him to steal more than $32,000 from his employer in hopes of earning the money back.

As is the case with most gamblers, however, he did not win the money back at the gambling tables, the company discovered the theft, and fired Parks.

Now unemployed, with gambling debt and an infant daughter, Parks had a lot of sleepless nights.

An upcoming trial for embezzling from his place of work didn't help matters.

When he slept, it was a deep sleep, according to a study in Psychology Today. So deep that he didn't have a clue what he was doing.

One early morning in May of that year, Kenneth drove to the home of his in-laws, Barbara Ann and Denis Woods, who lived in the Toronto suburb of Scarborough, to fix their furnace.

Once there, he grabbed a tire iron from the truck, used his key to enter the house, and went to his in-law's bedroom where he choked his father-in-law until he was unconscious then beat his mother-in-law with the tire iron and stabbed both of them with a kitchen knife.

He went upstairs to the teenage daughters' rooms, but stood there for a moment before running back down the stairs and leaving.

Afterwards, covered in blood, he drove to the police station, arriving at 4:45 a.m.

"I just killed someone with my bare hands; oh my God, I just killed someone; I've just killed two people; my God, I've just killed two people with my hands; my God, I've just killed two people. My hands; I just killed two people. I killed them; I just killed two people; I've just killed my mother- and father-in-law. I stabbed and beat them to death. It's all my fault," he said, seemingly in no pain despite some of the blood coming from tendons he'd sliced in both hands.

After a series of tests, including EEG scans that showed abnormal brain activity during deep sleep, experts determined that Kenneth had been sleepwalking, a defense that was cemented by his appearing to feel no pain when he arrived at the police station, despite his severe injuries.

Experts believed that he decided in his sleep that he was going to fix his in-law's furnace, then drove to the house, where he was startled by his in-laws. He attacked them without having a clue what he was doing.

Kenneth was acquitted, but it's possible that he was conscious the entire time, and suppressed his memories immediately because of the horror of what he had done.

In 1997, Arizona inventor Scott Falater stabbed his wife forty-four times and then dragged her outside to their swimming pool, holding her head underwater until she was dead.

"Are you saying to me my wife is dead?" Falater asked police, claiming that he was asleep throughout the entire ordeal.

According to one of the country's most esteemed sleep disorder experts, Dr. Rosalind Cartwright, killing while sleepwalking is a possibility.

"Sometimes they hurt themselves. Sometimes they hurt other people. But this is a state in which they are confused. They're not conscious. They think something terrible is happening, and they have to defend themselves, so often they will fight."

The 41-year-old Falater had a good job at Motorola and was active in the Mormon Church. According to his children, ages 12 and 15, their father went to bed at about 10 p.m., and their mother was on the couch reading a book.

An hour later, Falater's wife was dead.

A neighbor who called 911 said he saw Falater attempt to drown his wife in the pool.

Police had no motive for the crime.

"Usually you're able to find motive, and you're able to find out reasons behind an action. This one has remained a mystery. We don't know, and I don't know that we ever will," said Phoenix police Sgt. Mike Torres.

But police also said that Falater was aware enough of what he was doing to put on gloves before pushing his wife into the pool and later put both his clothes and the knife he used to stab his wife in a plastic container stashed in the trunk of his car.

Cartwright says even those acts are possible for sleepwalkers.

Prosecutors pointed out that Falater was aware enough to try to cover up the crime. He put on a pair of gloves before pushing his wife into the pool. And he put his clothes and the knife he used into a plastic container in the trunk of his car.

Sleep disorder experts say even that aspect of Falater's actions is possible while sleepwalking.

In court, Falater said, "Personally, it's something that's going to haunt me forever. There was no way I could do that, not intentionally. I loved her. I don't know what I would do without her."

The jury, however, didn't agree, and found him guilty of first-degree murder in his wife's death.

Falater could have received the death penalty, but instead was sentenced to life without the possibility of parole.

TEXAS FOOTBALL PARTY
TAKES A DEADLY TURN

It was meant to be an afternoon party spent eating, drinking, socializing with friends, and watching football.

The game? The Dallas Cowboys were playing their season opener against the New York Giants on September 10.

For Meredith Hight, 27, it was a chance to prove to herself, as well as the friends and colleagues at her home that day, that she could move on and be completely independent after what was looking to be a contentious divorce from her former husband, Spencer James Hight.

They had been living apart for months–Spencer Hight had moved out in March–although he had only just collected his personal items a few days before the football party.

In truth, Meredith Hight was handling things really well. And that is why her ex-husband lost it and crashed the party, a casual event thrown together in the Plano backyard of Meredith Hight.

He brought with him a gun, and by the party's end, eight people were dead, including Meredith Hight and her vengeful, spiteful, jealous soon-to-be-ex Spencer Hight.

Meredith's mother, Debbie Lane, believes that the party, which was the first event she had hosted since the divorce, caused her former husband to reel with jealousy, especially when he saw how easily she was readjusted to life without him.

Trouble brewing over money

Meredith met Spencer Hight when she transferred from a Georgia college to the University of Texas at Dallas, where she had plans to study math.

The two were neighbors until the close proximity grew into something more. They married in 2012.

At least the first four years were happy, if Meredith's Facebook posts are to be believed. She captioned a selfie of the two of them, "Pretty much what I live for," in 2015.

When Spencer Hight lost his job at Texas Instruments, however, things took a turn away from the blissful life that Meredith described.

While Meredith grew more and more frustrated that she was shouldering the entire burden of their home mortgage while her husband was out of work, Spencer grew more and more resentful of the emasculating fact that he was not the home's main breadwinner, at least not at the moment, while his busy wife was.

When Meredith filed for divorce, Spencer Hight had already been physically violent with her on two occasions, according to Lane.

His violent streak and his resentment only festered with the addition of alcohol.

A few days before the shooting, Spencer Hight sent depressed, telling texts to a friend, saying over and over again, "How can the one person you're supposed to love more than life itself end up being the one person you hate more than life itself?"

Revenge takes a violent turn

He took care of his hatred by making a stop at the party, to which he was not invited. He likely saw some of his friends there, and flew into a rage.

Neighbors reported hearing Spencer and Meredith Hight fighting before the gunshots began.

Crystal Sugg said she heard a man and a woman outside arguing, although she could only really hear bits and pieces of the argument, only that the woman was trying to go back into the house.

As she did, the man pulled out his gun and started shooting.

It was about 7:45 p.m.

"They were having a cookout that afternoon and they were getting prepared to watch the Cowboys football game," said Plano sheriff Gregory W. Rushkin, who said it was particularly disturbing to come upon multiple homicides at what moments before had been a party, which was a rarity for a city like Plano.

When it was over, police had arrived and killed the gunman, who had already fatally shot eight people. One of his victims survived the shooting.

The victims:

- Meredith Hight, 27. Hight was testing the waters as a newly-single woman by hosting a backyard barbecue with friends. She and Spencer Hight had separated after just over five years of marriage. Their wedding was in 2012, followed by a honeymoon in Jamaica. "I am completely heartbroken. The world lost the most beautiful, fierce, wicked smart, talented, witty, loving soul, wrote her longtime friend, Amanda Farr, on Facebook. "Meredith Hight, my oldest friend, you will be more than missed. You shaped my childhood, and I know your passing will forever shape my life. I love you, girl."

- Anthony Michael Cross, 33. Cross was a motion capture animator who lived in Dallas, where he worked on commercials and video games. He ran and worked out at the gym regularly,

- Olivia Nichole Diffner, 24. Diffner graduated Cum Laude with a Bachelor of Science degree in Marketing from the University of Texas at Dallas in 2015. She loved to travel and immersed herself in each new culture she visited.

- James Richard Dunlop, 29. Dunlop had been the best man at the Hights' wedding, and after Meredith and Spencer separated, he took Spencer in for a few months so he could get his bearings and find his own place to live.

- Darryl William Hawkins, 22. Hawkins' colleagues learned of his death when they went to his home to do a welfare check after their coworker hadn't turned up for work on Monday morning, only to find his place surrounded by yellow crime scene tape. Hawkins was a car salesman who worked at David McDavid Acura Plano.

- Rion Christopher Morgan, 21. Rion Morgan had been employed by the University of Texas at Dallas, where he was seen as an "exceptional employee and a warm, kind, generous colleague and friend." He had attended the Hights' wedding, and had spent the day before he died with his longtime friend, Spencer Hight. He had attended college with both of the couple.

- Myah Sade Bass, 28. Bass was a cosmetology student who both worked and studied at Tri-State Cosmetology Institute and Plano Community College. "She will be remembered as the angel that changed my cousin's life," said a family member of Bass's husband, Marcus Bass.

- Caleb Seth Edwards, 25. Edwards was an easygoing guy who was originally from Great Britain. He had plans to be a writer.

Two people at the party were not injured.

Spencer Hight was shot and killed by a responding officer.

"The first thing he heard was shots being fired. He saw people in the backyard that were down, that were shot. So, he instantly knew what was going on. He went into the house on his own," said Rushkin. "He made that decision that he couldn't wait for backup, for another partner, to go in as we were trained and go in to stop the shooter.

And that's exactly what he did. He actually found the shooter inside and ended his shooting spree."

The event devastated the community, located just outside of Dallas.

"We've never had a shooting of this magnitude, never had these many victims," said Rushkin. "It's just a terrible event."

Vigil held to bring peace, awareness

A candlelight vigil was held on September 13, as a way "to bring the community together, not only to pay respect to the victims that lost their lives, but also to raise awareness on family violence in the community," said Steve Stoler, director of media relations with the city of Plano. "Domestic violence is a problem everywhere, and it's by no means isolated to Plano. How do you turn something positive from such a terrible, horrific tragedy? I think the one thing you can do is raise awareness about the problem," he said.

In 2013, more than 1,600 women were killed by men in the United States, according to a study from the Violence Policy Center. Many of those women were victims of domestic violence. The weapon most often used was a gun.

FORMER CARPENTER SENTENCED IN DECADES-OLD MURDERS

Ultimately, it was the DNA that gave him away.

John Bittrolff, sentenced on September 12 to 50 years to life in prison, likely thought he had gotten away with more than one murder when 20 years went by and he wasn't arrested in the deaths of two prostitutes whose lives he took in late 1993 and early 1994, a three-month period of carnage.

It was the early days of DNA testing when the two bodies were found, but police determined that semen recovered from the women was from the same man.

It wasn't until DNA taken from Bittrolff's brother Timothy proved to be a partial match to that DNA, stored in a state database for decades, that there was a break in the case.

How the DNA proved a case

Timothy Bittrolff had been arrested for violating an order of protection, and because of mandatory collection laws, a mouth swab was taken and the sample entered into the DNA database.

A surprised Suffolk County homicide squad was notified that Timothy's DNA was a partial, familial match to that from the murder cases, which had almost grown cold.

The detectives asked the crime lab if they could narrow their findings further, and the lab responded with some interesting news.

"It's a sibling," Detective Charles Leser recalls the lab's response.

Because the DNA sample came from semen, they knew they were looking for a brother. Timothy Bittrolff had two, John Bittrolff and Kevin Bittrolff.

They saw John, who would have been 27 at the time of the murders, as the more likely suspect, but put both men under surveillance in hopes of obtaining something with a DNA sample, such as a discarded cigarette with saliva.

John almost immediately realized he was being tailed, despite the undercover vehicle of choice being a plumber's van.

"From day one, he knew we were following him," Leser said, adding that he worked hard to evade them and would watch them from job sites to see where they were.

"I think in the back of his mind, he was nervous," Leser added. "He never discarded something personal."

When a tossed cigarette from Kevin, who would have been 21 at the time of the murders, was determined to be another partial hit, detectives focused exclusively on John Bittrolff, watching him drink beer inside his home in hopes of him throwing something useful in the trash.

"That never happened," Leser said. "He had tons of beer bottles. I don't know what he did with them."

The detectives finally took a roundabout way to get the evidence they needed and obtained three DNA samples from the Bittrolff trash, that of the suspect's wife and their two sons, and sent it for testing.

"If you take the female DNA and the suspect DNA, they make the two kids," Leser said. "It's like a paternity test."

Bittrolff was stopped in July of 2013 on his way to work and agreed to accompany officers to the police station for questioning.

Bittrolff says he's innocent

Despite the DNA evidence, as well as wood chips and paint that would have been materials consistent with someone working in construction, Bittrolff proclaimed his innocence from the time of his arrest, when he made his first phone call to his wife.

He later protested the charges during an interrogation by police.

Retired Det. John McLeer of the Suffolk County Police Department began questioning Bittrolff by telling him they were investigating the murders of two prostitutes.

"Really," Bittrolff said. "Interesting."

"Have you ever used the services of a prostitute?" Detective Sergeant Charles Leser then asked.

"No, never," Bittrolff replied. "I can get laid any time I want. I don't want to bring disease home to my wife."

Bittrolff married his wife, Patricia Asero, in 1995, but the two had dated for ten years prior to the wedding, and lived together beginning in 1993, the year of the first murder.

The two detectives then showed photos of Tangredi and McNamee to Bittrolff, taken both when they were alive and when they were found, posed naked, their heads brutally bashed in.

"I have no idea who she is," Bittrolff said of Tangredi, and "I don't know her," he said of McNamee.

When Leser told Bittrolff that semen found on the victims had been linked to him, he said, "To me? Really? It surprises me, yes, because it's not me."

Leser told him about the results from his trash, and he asked for a lawyer.

"There's no way," Bittrolff told detectives. "End the conversation there, because now I need a lawyer."

He then called his wife, whose name is tattooed on his arm.

"Hello, it's me. I got arrested," Bittrolff said in that call. "I'm not kidding you. I'm dead serious. Two murders. From 1993. Two prostitutes. They're saying they found my semen in them."

Detectives then offered Bittrolff something to drink, thereby securing a cup to directly confirm the DNA match they already had.

"It all matched," Leser said.

After 20 years, due to a stroke of good luck, they had their guy.

"The fish just happened to jump in the boat," added lead prosecutor Robert Biancavilla, Suffolk County Assistant District Attorney. "The killer left his calling card on both girls. He didn't realize that he also left his genetic fingerprints on the victims."

Authorities knew they had the right man. Now they just had to prove it to a jury.

Questions arise over Bittrolff's guilt

People who know Bittrolff were surprised after learning of his arrest for the murders of two dead prostitutes.

"Whenever I needed him, he always helped everybody," one man said. "It's just unbelievable. Nobody can believe it. He's like the mayor of this town. He knows everybody. He helps everybody out."

But prosecutors say DNA supports their version of events, despite Bittrolff's protests and neighbors' surprise.

"It happens," said Suffolk County District Attorney Thomas Spota. "We don't know everything of the dark side of people's lives, but again, we present our evidence and we'll leave it up to the jury."

The Manorville, New York, carpenter, a husband with two children, was 48 when he was arrested and charged with two counts of second-degree murder in the deaths of Rita Tangredi, 41, and Colleen McNamee, 20.

He is also a possible suspect in the deaths of at least ten other Long Island-area prostitutes whose bodies were found near those of Tangredi and McNamee, whose bodies were discovered about 13 miles apart in wooded areas of Long Island, an idyllic place that seems too sun-swept and beautiful, the Atlantic breezes too briny, to be a site for murder.

Tangredi was troubled but loved

"My sister was a somebody," said Diane Santacroce, Rita Tangredi's older sister, who prayed every day for 21 years that her troubled sibling's killer would be found. "She was a mother, a sister, a daughter. She wasn't just somebody to be thrown away."

The youngest of six kids, Tangredi was athletic and fearless, which allowed her to excel in sports, including soccer and kickball.

One Christmas, one of their brothers received a unicycle for Christmas, and Tangredi, who was just 7 or 8, quickly dominated.

"Boom, she was riding it," Santacroce said. "She was amazing. She was fearless."

Tangredi attended Brentwood Junior High School until freshman year, when she dropped out and "was out doing what she wanted to do," Santacroce said.

That included a period of drug addiction, which had gotten much worse in the years prior to her death.

"There were quite a lot of interventions," Santacroce said. "Everyone tried to help her. It's a difficult thing."

Tangredi was the maid of honor at her sister's 1978 wedding, although the two later lost touch when Santacroce moved to Florida.

Tangredi, who was 31 when she died, was last seen hitchhiking on Montauk Highway in November 1993. The mother of three children was found a day later, partially buried November 2, 1993, in an abandoned housing development in East Patchogue.

McNamee was getting her life back on track when she disappeared

McNamee, just 20 when she was murdered, was pretty with curly auburn hair that just brushed her shoulders.

She was not without her troubles, however.

Arrested once on charges of loitering for the purposes of prostitution, she was also struggling with substance abuse and was attending regular drug rehab sessions in order to get clean.

She was headed to a drug rehabilitation center South Shore Treatment Center in Islandia, where she was an outpatient, when she left her Holbrook home on Long Island for the last time on January 5, 1994.

It was just a 15-minute drive from home.

Because of her newfound strength, she had hope for her future after some early bumps in her own personal road.

"On her last day, her life was in order, she was happy. She was dressed so beautifully," her mother, Charlotte, said in 1996.

McNamee was last seen in front of the Blue Dawn Diner, a victim of progress that is also now gone, hitching a ride in a small blue car that drove east on Veterans Memorial Highway.

She was found January 30, 1994, in the brush alongside Express Drive South. She was naked, she'd been beaten and raped, and her body was posed, her arms above her head and her legs spread wide apart, robbing her of any final dignity by leaving her so exposed.

It rattled those who knew her, including her neighbor, Sal D'Aguanno, who had lived two houses down from the small white house where McNamee grew up.

"She was a pretty girl, outgoing, and a nice kid," said D'Aguanno, who unfortunately found himself at the crime scene as a photographer for Suffolk County police.

The girl who had delivered newspapers from her bicycle and graduated from Sachem High School in 1991 no longer had a chance to ensure her life stayed on track.

She had been robbed of her future by someone who was able to hide in plain sight for 20 years, living his life.

"Bittrolff picked these women because they were vulnerable," said prosecutor Robert Biancavilla. "He picked them because he thought no one cared about them. But there were people who cared about these girls. And for over 20 years, he got away with this."

At trial, both sides focused on DNA

According to defense attorney William Keahon, the DNA that officials were able to trace back to Bittrolff thanks to his brother's arrest was not enough proof that he strangled and bludgeoned both women, whose injuries were so severe that their brains were exposed.

"The DNA in this case is not proof of murder," Keahon said. "They want you to assume that because he had sex with these two women, he must have killed them. And if you have to assume something, you don't know if it's true."

Biancavilla, on the other hand, said the semen was the only evidence the prosecution needed to convict their suspect.

"It means he killed them," Biancavilla said. "What other explanation is there that both women ended up dead, with their brains bashed in, shortly after having sex with John Bittrolff? There is no other explanation."

Jury finds Bittrolff guilty

Because the media headlines read "father" and "prostitutes," it would not have come as a surprise if a jury had determined that the lives of two women believed to be streetwalkers weren't all that important compared to a hard-working father of two, but a jury found Bittrolff guilty of two counts of second-degree murder, despite his protests that he wasn't involved.

After the trial, Biancavilla told reporters that Bittrolff not only hated women but was also a savage, brutal hunter who had once wrestled a pig to the ground to slit its throat, and cut the heart out of a deer he'd shot and ate it raw while still in the woods, blood dripping down his chin.

He also said that he believed that other Long Island murder victims could be the handiwork of the former carpenter.

"I suspect there are other victims out there. This is behavior that he's comfortable with," he said. "He's got a long history of brutality and disregard for life."

The defense, however, had another story.

"From day one in this case until now, Mr. Bittrolff has said one thing—that he did not do this," Defense attorney Jonathan Manley said, saying the defense planned to file an appeal.

Family finally allowed to voice their sorrow

At Bittrolff's sentencing hearing, the family members of Rita and Colleen McNamee "What do you say to the person who killed your mother?" asked Tangredi's son, Anthony Beller. "Forgiveness—I do hold some forgiveness for you, John Bittrolff. But I also believe in justice."

Beller was 11 when his mother disappeared, and he has since been given what will be the difficult task of attempting to explain to his children what happened to their grandmother so many years ago.

"I will one day have to tell my children how their grandmother was taken from us. You are the monster in that story," Beller said. "All I see is an unremorseful animal."

178

The family of Colleen McNamee was no less forthright when facing down their loved one's killer, who sat silently in the courtroom as they spoke.

"You're a liar. You're an animal. You're a disease to society, a killer who will always pose a threat to society," said Thomas McNamee Jr., one of Colleen's brothers.

"My daughter's hopes and ambitions, and our hopes for her, died with her," said McNamee's father, Lawrence McNamee Sr., who asked Suffolk County Supreme Court Justice Richard Ambro to "consider not only the killing, but the brutality and the showmanship" of the murders when handing down the sentence.

"These two murders are as brutal as anything I've ever seen," Ambro said, giving the 51-year-old man two consecutive sentences of 25 years to life for the murders, a sentence with a goal to ensure that Bittrolff would die behind bars.

"These families had hoped that someday they would turn their lives around," Ambro told Bittrolff. "You crushed their skulls, strangled them and left them naked in the cold woods. You are evil, Mr. Bittrolff."

Bittrolff again said nothing.

Aftermath

Bittrolff could also be a suspect in the murder of a third woman, Sandra Costilla, who was found dead 18 days after Rita Tangredi's body was found, approximately two days after she was murdered.

Costilla, a Hispanic woman from Queens, was not a prostitute, but according to those who knew her, lived a similar lifestyle.

Her cause of death was also similar, as was the way her body was positioned when it was found.

It was unclear whether or not authorities were unable to establish

DNA evidence in the murder of Costilla, who was identified by her fingerprints.

He is imprisoned at Downstate Correctional Facility, a maximum-security prison in Fishkill, New York.

The other 10 murders that have been attributed to the unidentified Long Island Serial Killer but could be the work of Bittrolff, were from both Suffolk and Nassau counties, and were found by a cadaver dog near Gilgo Beach.

"That investigation is continuing," Biancavilla said.

Others, however, have said there is no evidence linking Bittrolff to the Gilgo Beach murders.

CONCERT ENDS IN WORST
SHOOTING IN U.S. HISTORY

Stephen Paddock spent almost a week fine-tuning the details of his murder spree. It was his third attempt, and this time, he planned to get it right.

Paddock had in August booked a room in Chicago overlooking Grant Park, where the four-day Lollapalooza festival has been held annually since 2005. This year's lineup included Lorde, Blink-182, Machine Gun Kelly, Foster the People and hundreds of other acts, but he never checked in. Paddock also skipped out on a reservation at a downtown Las Vegas Airbnb for the Life Is Beautiful festival, a three-day festival that featured a lineup similar to Lollapalooza.

This time, he was ready.

The 64-year-old from Mesquite, Nevada, checked into a comped room at the Mandalay Bay hotel on September 25, but moved to a suite on the 32nd floor three days later. His new room–"He was given the room for free because he was a good customer," according to reports from the Associated Press–overlooked Las Vegas Village, which was slated to host a three-day country music festival that would feature headlining act Jason Aldean, the last show on the bill.

His window was 400 meters from the stage, and his vantage point was perfectly suited for large-scale destruction.

He then apparently placed the "Do not disturb" sign on the door, then spent more than 48 hours putting plans for his deadly rampage at the popular Route 92 Harvest Festival, an annual Las Vegas tradition, into motion.

According to Clark County Sheriff Joe Lombardo, Paddock had carried more than 10 suitcases into his suite, the same suite where

Jeff Bridges had in stayed a year earlier, marveling on a video he posted for fans over the amazing view he had of Las Vegas Village below.

Why he did it, however, may go unanswered forever.

"We have no idea what his belief system was," said Lombardo, who remained calm during press conferences in the days following the tragic incident that decimated his city. "I can't get into the mind of a psychopath at this point."

Those suitcases carried 23 firearms, numerous high-capacity magazines that could hold up to 100 rounds and scads of ammunition. Weapons included four DDM4 rifles, three FN-15 rifles, one AR-15, an AR-10 and a handgun. Two of the rifles were equipped with sights and were mounted on bipods, giving Paddock more precision and stability while shooting.

Carnage and chaos

Just as the music festival was coming to an end, at about 10 p.m. on October 1, while people were completely immersed in the music, Paddock broke his hotel room window–"We believe he had a device similar to a hammer to smash the window," Lombardo said–and raised one of his rifles.

Country superstar Jason Aldean, who has had 19 singles top the charts including "Big Green Tractor," "Don't You Want to Stay" (a duet with Kelly Clarkson) and "Night Train," among many others, was playing the last show of the festival and was a half-hour into his show when the first gunshots were heard on the Las Vegas Strip, sending the country music singer and his crew flying to take cover.

With 22,000 people in front of the stage, "it was like shooting fish in a barrel," one singer said.

Paddock was using bump fire stocks, which give semi-automatic weapons the same speed as automatic weapons. With the stocks, he was able to fire at a rate of 90 bullets in 10 seconds, authorities said.

There were 12 bump sticks in Paddock's room, which allowed him to methodically spray the entire area in front of the stage, leaving a bloody swath of destruction.

"There was this onslaught of shots," said concertgoer Brian Claypool in an interview with MSNBC. "It felt like World War III. It felt like it would never end."

People were "frozen" in shock, said Claypool, who began dragging people to the ground to protect them from the bullets that were seemingly everywhere.

In footage released after the incident, the shots were fired rapidly and steadily while people screamed in terror as they realized what they initially thought were fireworks were anything but.

"Everybody starts running, everyone's on the ground, everybody's yelling, everyone's confused," added survivor Sara Hass. "No one knows what's really going on. Everyone thought it might have been fireworks, but it was...you know."

The scene was like something from a horror movie as people scrambled to safety, leaping over concrete barriers in an effort to escape.

It was, witnesses said, a stampede.

"Everybody started kind of like charging our direction and we were standing there just dancing and we weren't understanding and then you can hear that machine gun like, I can't even, that was the worst. And then everybody is running and screaming and I mean there is people trampling people," said Megan Urfer.

"Everyone had to fall on top of each other whether they were alive or not, basically, because every time someone got up, the shooting would start," another witness added.

Shooter was calm amid the chaos

As people raced for safety, uncertain where the shooter was located, Paddock was calmly trading weapons while hidden behind the curtain, the white fabric fluttered each time he took aim with a new rifle stock.

"The gunshots lasted for 10 to 15 minutes. It didn't stop," witness Rachel de Kerf told CNN.

Singer Jake Owen was onstage, about 50 feet from Aldean, when the first shots rang out.

"It was kind of the thing where like, 'Is that gunfire?'" he said in an interview with the Today Show. "And it got faster and faster. It sounded like it was an automatic rifle. You could hear it ringing off the tops of the rafters on the stage. That's when you saw people fleeing, and at that point everyone on stage just started running everywhere possible, and it was pretty chaotic for sure. There was blood on people and you could see a couple folks on the street that had, that looked, like they'd been shot, lying there."

Paddock fired for approximately 10 minutes from the time the first 911 call came in at 10:08 p.m., and by the time he was done, 58 people were dead and more than 500 were injured.

Could a faster response have led to fewer deaths?

A minute before the clock struck 10 p.m. (and almost 10 minutes before the mass shooting would begin) unarmed security guard Jesus Campos heard what he described as "drilling noises" coming from Paddock's suite on the 32nd floor, seconds before Paddock fired at him through the door, shooting him three times.

Campos had been on patrol when he was asked to check a door on the 32nd floor. When he got there, he was unable to enter the floor via the stairwell, which had been barricaded.

"There was metal bracket holding the door in place. That was just out of the ordinary," he said in the only interview he gave, on "The Ellen DeGeneres Show."

Campos reported the blocked door to dispatch, which sent one of the building's engineers to investigate, then used the elevator to access the 32nd floor.

It was then that he heard the drilling noises, and assumed there was construction work going on in the area.

Campos checked out the metal bracket on the door, which had only prevented the door from being opened from the other side. As it closed, it made a loud noise that Campos believes caught Paddock's attention, causing him to fire into the hall.

"As I was walking down, I heard rapid fire. And at first, I took cover. I felt a burning sensation. I went to go lift my pant leg up and I saw the blood. That's when I called it in on my radio that shots have been fired," Campos said.

From the doorway where he had taken cover, Campos warned the engineer who had been sent up to check the jammed door, as well as a guest who had come out of another room.

The building engineer, Stephen Schuck, thought he was hearing a jackhammer when he heard Campos yelling for him to take cover.

"Within milliseconds, if he didn't say that, I would have got hit," said Schuck, who told DeGeneres that he could feel the bullets as they whistled past his head.

A few minutes after shooting Campos, Paddock turned his attention to the crowd below.

The security guard is still struggling with the after-effects of his close brush with death, and canceled several scheduled interviews before going off the grid completely, until his interview with DeGeneres.

Questions about the timeline surrounding the shooting have not made the situation any easier.

"I'm doing better each day, slowly but surely. Just healing mentally and physically," he said.

Were police slow to respond?

Initially, police credited Campos with bringing the shooting to an end by distracting Paddock in the hallway, stopping him from continuing his assault on the country music fans below.

They then later retracted that statement, when it was revealed that Campos had radioed in that there had been shots fired at 9:59 p.m.

There were numerous police on hand at the event, not only outside to monitor the crowd of 22,000, but also inside Mandalay Bay, where officers were attending an event.

Not only had hotel security been alerted when Campos radioed in, Schuck – saved from being shot by the warning from Campos – also issued a radio alert.

According to transcripts, he said: "Call the police, someone's firing a gun up here, someone's firing a rifle on the 32nd floor down the hallway."

While Schuck was not sure what room the shots were coming from, it should have been obvious when police arrived, since Paddock had placed a wheeled cart outside of the door to his room, with wires running from the cart to somewhere underneath Paddock's door.

While the cart was armed with three cameras Paddock had set up to monitor activity outside his hotel suite, it could have been an elaborate booby trap to prevent police from breaching his hotel room until his lust for death was satisfied.

For those racing to escape the hail of gunfire below, the timeline must have felt excruciatingly slow.

According to the Las Vegas Metropolitan Police Department, at

10:17 p.m., 18 minutes after Campos was shot, the first officers arrived on the 32nd floor.

Campos, told the officers which room was Paddock's, and after eight more officers were called to the scene, they began evacuating guests and searching the other rooms on the floor.

At 10:24, officers grouped near Paddock's room, 25 minutes after he fired his first shot.

After Paddock fired on officers, they called for a SWAT team, and waited for reinforcements.

Meanwhile, an active shooter alert was released, and at 10:25 p.m., taxi drivers were warned by a police alert to avoid the Mandalay Bay area.

Still, it would be almost another hour before officers entered room 135.

When they did, they found 23 guns and thousands of rounds of ammunition and three cameras, but no booby trap on the cart outside the room.

Paddock was dead from a self-inflicted gunshot wound to the head.

Many lives will be forever changed

Country singer Jason Aldean sang for a few seconds more after the shooting began, his 2012 song "When She Says Baby," uncertain like everyone else at the show of exactly what it was he was hearing.

When he did realize, he and his bandmates stopped mid-song and left the stage.

"Jason's band and crew hid behind the equipment once they realized what was happening," a source told US magazine. "The band's bus was also in line of fire and has bullet holes."

For Aldean, a two-time winner of the Academy of Country Music's Entertainer of the Year Award, the words came painfully.

"Tonight has been beyond horrific. I still don't know what to say but wanted to let everyone know that me and my crew are safe. My thoughts and prayers go out to everyone involved tonight. It hurts my heart that this would happen to anyone who was just coming out to enjoy what should have been a fun night," wrote Aldean on Twitter after the incident.

The concert lineup had featured 35 acts slated to perform over the three-day event at Sin City's Mandalay Bay Resort, including Eric Church, Jake Owen, Big and Rich, Maren Morris, Midland, Sam Hunt and Ashley McBryde.

"We were in the middle of it," Owen said. "When the shots started being fired and you could hear it ricocheting off the roof of the stage, we started just running in any direction we could. You didn't know where it was coming from… At one point I was sitting on the ground behind a car with about 20 other people crouched down behind a car, just the fear in everyone's eyes but yet the feeling of everyone looking for someone to make sure they were okay. I've just never experienced anything like it before."

For 10 minutes, Las Vegas became a battlefield.

Mike Cronk, a retired teacher, said he and other bystanders helped keep his friend who had been shot three times alive.

"We kept him conscious," Cronk said. "He actually, you know, had his finger in one of the holes and we were like, 'OK, keep your finger in there.' Then we got off shirts and stuff to try and keep it compressed."

Forbes Riley was on his balcony 16 floors above Paddock's suite when the shooting started.

"We were on the balcony last night taking photos, and like everyone's reported, we thought we were all hearing fireworks. There were people strewn everywhere and we thought, 'Oh, that just can't be real.'"

They, like others, soon realized how very wrong they were.

"All of a sudden we heard about three or four little pop, pop, pops, and everybody looked around and said, 'Oh, it's just firecrackers,'" said Gail Davis, who was attending the concert with her husband. "And then we heard pop, pop, pop, and it just kept going and going, and my husband said, 'That's not firecrackers. That sounds like a semi-automatic rifle.' And then everybody started screaming and started to run."

It was, Davis said, a war zone.

"I looked over to my right where this girl had been standing right beside me," she said. "First, she stood there and she grabbed her stomach and she looked at her hands and her hands were all bloody, and she was wearing, like, a little crop top and, you know, blue jean shorts and cowboy boots, and she looked at her hands and her hands were bloody, and she just kind of screamed and she just fell back."

The shooting slowed when the stage lights were turned off, making it more difficult for Paddock to see his targets, but still, the carnage was significant.

Who was the man behind the massacre?

So, who was Stephen Paddock, and what drove him to let loose with a spray of bullets that left unimaginable carnage along the Las Vegas strip?

According to police, Paddock had no criminal record or any reported strange behavior before going off the rails and leaving a nation in turmoil.

The night before the shooting, though Paddock was clearly nervous.

He made two noise complaints about a downstairs neighbor, who was playing country music.

Albert Garzon said he turned down the music after the first

complaint, at 1:30 a.m., then turned it off when security guards arrived at his door the second time.

He had no idea that Paddock was the person who complained about the noise, until Monday morning, when he realized that the room above his was the one with the windows shot out.

"I looked up and I could see his curtain flapping in the wind," Garzon said.

What do we know about Paddock?

Stephen Paddock, a retired accountant, was 64 and lived in Mesquite, Nevada, about 80 miles northeast of Las Vegas.

He was twice divorced with no children, and was currently living in Mesquite with his girlfriend, Marilou Danley, a woman he met while she was working as a hostess

Las Vegas gunman Stephen Paddock was obsessed with his status when it came to being one of the city's elite, but when he started losing large amounts of cash, that popularity was quickly replaced with depression—which investigators say might be one of the primary reasons behind his attack on October 1.

Clark County Sheriff Joe Lombardo talked extensively about the mass shooting, Paddock and the changing timeline, which has led to controversy and questions regarding the sniping attack, in a two-hour interview with KLAS, a local CBS affiliate in Las Vegas.

Lombardo said Paddock had a long history of ups and downs with money but he "lost a significant amount of his wealth" since September 2015, which may have been behind the horrific mass murder he perpetrated.

He graduated from California State University, Northridge in 1977, with a degree in business administration.

While getting his degree, he worked for the federal government as a letter carrier for the U.S. Postal Service, a job he began in 1975.

Later, he worked as an agent for the Internal Revenue Service and as an auditor for the Defense Contract Audit Agency.

He also worked for the company that later became Lockheed Martin, a United States-based defense contractor with global ties.

"Stephen Paddock worked for a predecessor company of Lockheed Martin from 1985 until 1988," the company told ABC in a statement. "We're cooperating with authorities to answer questions they may have about Mr. Paddock and his time with the company."

Stephen Paddock seemingly had only two passions, gambling and flying.

He was a regular at a Mesquite bar, where he played video poker while throwing back shots of tequila. (His love of tequila shots was evident in the main photo circulated by the media after the shooting, in which Paddock, wearing a drab plaid shirt unbuttoned to reveal a white undershirt beneath, had his eyes closed, a shot glass in his hand.)

He also had his pilot's license, and owned a plane that he kept at Mesquite Metro Airport in Texas between 2007 to 2009.

"I do not recall that he was ever a person who created any problems for us," the airport's director told ABC News. "He kept his accounts up to date, and we never had any problems with him here." And although his father had a long criminal record, the younger Paddock, the oldest of four boys, had no criminal history.

"We checked the federal and local databases and state databases," said Lombardo. "We had no knowledge of this individual."

His family was equally surprised by the incident.

"We have no idea how or why this happened," said the youngest brother, Eric Paddock. "As far as we know, Steve was perfectly fine. Steve had nothing to do with any political organization, religious organization, no white supremacist, nothing."

The news of his brother's murderous rampage was like being "crushed by an asteroid," Eric Paddock said.

Like father, like son?

Sometimes, genetics and evil go hand in hand, and Paddock may have been continuing the legacy left by his late father, Benjamin Hoskins Paddock, a diagnosed psychopath who spent eight years on the FBI's Ten Most Wanted list, from 1969 to 1977.

In 2010, London-based journalist Philip Hunter delved into the idea of a genetic connection between psychopaths in "The Psycho Gene," which appeared in the scientific journal EMBO Reports.

And although there is no definite proof that a psychopath is more likely to pass on such traits to a child, it is something being talked about in scientific circles, which has isolated the MAOA gene, called "the warrior gene" because those who carry it have lower levels of the feel-good chemicals dopamine and serotonin, and are more prone to aggression and violence.

"Psychopathy does seem to be heritable, and appears to have its basis at least in part in 'biological' factors linked to basic emotional systems, so that the mature psychopath never develops a complete set of pro-social emotions like empathy, guilt, and the ability to truly care about and for others," said Richard Wiebe, who studies the link between psychology and criminology at Fitchburg State College in Fitchburg, Massachusetts.

There are also certain genetic markers that have been connected to psychopathic behavior, although that doesn't mean that people with those markers are destined to a life of crime, nor does having the genetic markers absolve anyone of criminal behavior.

"Nothing relieves one of the obligation to behave civilized," said Anthony Walsh of the Criminal Justice Department at Boise State University in Idaho.

Con man father was not in the picture

The elder Paddock, born in bucolic Sheboygan, Wisconsin, a blue-collar community along the shores of Lake Michigan, was a bank robber and con man who initially seemed to be living on the straight and narrow.

He served as a Seaman Second Class in the United States Navy during World War II before a string of car thefts landed him in the Illinois State Penitentiary (the future home of John Wayne Gacy, Richard Speck and Leopold and Loeb) for six years.

After he got out, Paddock married Dolores Irene Hudson in 1952. The couple had four sons, Stephen, born in 1953, Patrick, born in 1957, Bruce, born in 1959, and Eric, born in 1960.

Just after Stephen's birth, however, Paddock had conned the wrong people and written a few bad checks, enough to earn a few more years behind bars.

When he got out, he opened a service station in Tucson, Arizona, where he also sold used cars, but bad decisions followed him across state lines.

After a string of bank robberies that netted him just over $25,000, he was finally arrested again in 1960, just after the birth of his youngest son, but not before attempting to evade an FBI agent who was pursuing him by attempting to run him over with his car. This time, he was sentenced to 20 years in prison, but six years in, he escaped from La Tuna Federal Correctional Institute in Anthony, Texas, and moved to Oregon, where he lived under an assumed name, Bruce Warner Erickson.

There, Paddock ran a bingo parlor to benefit the Center for Education Reform, a non-profit organization until he was arrested in 1978. After he was released on parole, he lived in Texas with a girlfriend, racking up one final racketeering charge for bingo operations, for which he paid a $100,000 fine to avoid jail time.

His children, however, did not spend time with their father, even when he was not in jail.

According to youngest son Eric, their mother told the boys their father was dead, and Stephen stepped in to fill that role for his siblings.

"Steve was like a dad surrogate. He took me camping," Eric told New York Magazine. "I liked my brother. He was a good guy."

That goodness, however, obviously didn't last. And as it happens, Stephen was not the only Paddock brother to run afoul of the law.

Bruce Paddock had a thing for kiddie porn

On October 27, third-born brother Bruce Paddock, 58, pleaded not guilty to 20 counts of possession of child pornography in a Los Angeles courtroom after he was arrested two days earlier at the Los Angeles Assisted Living Home in North Hollywood.

He faces felony charges of being in possession of more than 600 images of child pornography, including at least 10 images of a minor under 12 years old.

The materials were found at a business in Sun Valley, where Bruce Paddock had been squatting until he was discovered and evicted. Afterwards, his stash of porn was discovered.

He was eventually tracked down at the assisted living facility, where he was living due to his health. When he was arrested by a task force that also included the FBI, he was in a wheelchair.

The investigation into Bruce Paddock, who is being held on a $600,000 bond, began long before Stephen Paddock's Oct. 1 murderous rampage.

According to the criminal complaint, Bruce Paddock's alleged crimes occurred in 2014.

Before his arrest, he spoke to reporters about his brother.

"I don't know how he could stoop to this low point, hurting someone else," Bruce Paddock – whose criminal record includes vandalism, theft and criminal threats - told NBC News. "It wasn't suicide by cop since he killed himself. He killed a bunch of people and then killed himself so he didn't have to face whatever it was."

He also spoke to his neighbors in the retirement community, reportedly bragging about his brother being the Las Vegas shooter.

That prompted neighbors to alert authorities, suggesting that they might want to look into Bruce Paddock as well.

When they did, they found the outstanding warrant from 2014 on child pornography charges.

Brain study may yield clues

It's possible that genetics did play a role in Paddock's actions, and researchers at Stanford hope to find out.

His brain is being sent to neuropathologist Dr. Hannes Vogel, who studies more than 200 brains a year.

"Something broke in his head is the only thing possible," said Eric Paddock. "Did he have a stroke? I'm hoping they cut open his brain and find something. There's a data point missing."

According to scientists, changes in brain chemistry – or existing brain chemistry, such as the presence of the MAOA gene – could have contributed to Paddock's actions that October night.

"If it's possible to gain insight into his actions at the biological level, we might be in a better position to fend off such tragedies in the future," David Eagleman, director of Stanford's Center for Science and the Law, wrote in an essay for CNN.

Marilou Danley had no idea

Several weeks before the shooting, Stephen Paddock bought his girlfriend, 62-year-old Marilou Danley, a ticket to the Philippines.

"Stephen told me he found a cheap ticket for me to the Philippines and that he wanted me to take a trip home to see my family," she said in a statement.

Once she was there, he wired her $100,000, a gift that came as a complete surprise, and led her to believe he was breaking up with her. She had no idea that it was a sign that he was planning such a horrific act of violence.

Eric Paddock saw the money as a way for his brother to take care of the woman he loved, knowing that he wouldn't see her again.

Police initially believed that Danley, who met Paddock when she was working as a hostess at the Atlantic Casino in Reno, was involved in the incident, but she is cooperating with police.

Although Danley was married at the time, and had been since 1990, she left her husband and moved in with Paddock in 2013. She divorced her husband, Geary Danley, in 2015.

Eric Paddock said the two loved each other dearly.

"They were adorable — big man, tiny woman. He loved her. He doted on her," he said.

The same could be said of Danley, who adapted to her boyfriend's many allergies – including the chemicals in perfumes, hair sprays and cleaning products as well as blood pressure medication, which prevented him from renewing his pilot's license - as best she could.

"The reason Marilou looks so plain in that picture they keep posting of her is because for him she would not wear perfumes or hair sprays or anything with scents in it because it affected him," Eric said.

But Eric may have been seeing the relationship through rose-colored glasses – along with love for the brother he thought of like a father.

According to employees at the Starbucks located inside the Virgin River Casino in Reno, where Paddock and Danley frequently stopped when they gambled, there was a sense of dread that came over the store when the two entered the doors.

"He would glare down at her and say — with a mean attitude — 'You don't need my casino card for this. I'm paying for your drink, just like I'm paying for you.' Then she would softly say, 'okay' and step back behind him. He was so rude to her in front of us," the store supervisor, Esperanza Mendoza, told the Los Angeles Times.

Guns were not Paddock's passion

According to his brother, Eric Paddock, Stephen was "not an avid gun guy at all."

Instead, he was into gambling, which is why he met his girlfriend there, and why the couple were so easily recognized at the Reno casino's Starbucks.

"The fact that he had those kind of weapons is ... just ... where the hell did he get automatic weapons? He has no military background or anything like that. "He's a guy who lived in a house in Mesquite and drove down and gambled in Las Vegas," Eric said.

Survivors struggle to regain their lives

Kim Gervais never imagined that a trip to see her favorite musicians would end with a doctor telling her three weeks later, "This is your life. You're a quadriplegic."

Gervais had attended the music festival with two friends – Dana Smith and Pati Mestas, three grandmothers who relished in the opportunity to relive their youth.

Mestas died, and Gervais was hit in the back by a bullet. Only Smith was left uninjured.

"I'm disgusted," said Gervais, who had lived an active life – she had raised her two daughters alone after her sprint car racer husband was killed in a crash - and ran a business servicing trash compactors.

"I'm angered, I have all kinds of emotions toward him. Because he took a part of me that I can't get back."

Smith, who had been friends with the other two women for more than 20 years, may not have been physically injured, but emotionally, well, that's a different story.

She doesn't sleep and doesn't eat, and spends her nights watching videos of the incident, unable to shake the horror of it all.

"Three of us went," she said. "And I left one in the morgue and one in the hospital."

Mostly, she spends her days in bed. There is, she said, "nothing to get me going."

An aide at a local high school, 52-year-old Smith has not returned to work for fear that the popping of milk cartons, a student ritual at lunchtime, will send her into a panic attack.

Gervais, Smith and the family of their friend who died, are just a few of the people whose lives are forever transformed by Paddock's actions on the night of October 1.

Husbands and wives mourn the loss of their spouses, parents mourn for their children, children grieve the loss of their parents, and a nation works to stay strong in the face of yet another tragedy.

According to Dr. Bryan Tsao, chair of the neurology department at Loma Linda University Health, the aftermath can be grim for survivors.

"We all kind of forget that these people have to live with it for the rest of their lives. Those that I've seen that cannot — that cannot stop dwelling on the tragedy of it, on the injustice of it, on their permanent disability — they don't do well. They take the struggle and kind of go down a different road."

Incident sparks gun debate

Some survivors lamented that no one shot back at Paddock after witnesses determined where the shooter was.

"The biggest problem for me and for many was that we didn't hear anybody returning fire," said survivor Rusty Dees. "I'm very concerned that we had no one outside to protect us."

Others, however, pointed out just how risky shooting back would have been.

"I've been a proponent of the 2nd Amendment my entire life," wrote Josh Abbott Band guitarist Caleb Keeter. "Until the events of last night. I cannot express how wrong I was. We actually have members of our crew with CHL licenses, and legal firearms on the bus. They were useless. We couldn't touch them for fear police might think we were part of the massacre and shoot us.

"One man laid waste to a city with fearless, dedicated police officers desperately trying to help, because of access to an insane amount of fire power," he added. "Enough is enough.... We need gun control RIGHT. NOW. My biggest regret is that I stubbornly didn't realize it until my brothers on the road and myself were threatened by it. That being said, I'll not live in fear of anyone. We will regroup, we'll come back, and we'll rock your fucking faces off. Bet on it."

The aftermath

For survivors of the Las Vegas shooting, the death threats that have been appearing on social media are almost as bad as the event itself.

Like Holocaust deniers or those who suggested that the Sandy Hook shooting that left 16 children dead was also a hoax, are suggesting that the Las Vegas incident was staged by the government, perhaps as a distraction from the current political climate.

"You are a lying piece of shit and I hope someone truly shoots you in the head," one person wrote in a Facebook message to Canadian

Braden Matejka, who suffered a gunshot wound to the head but survived in the event that left 58 people dead.

"Your soul is disgusting and dark! You will Pay for the consequences," wrote another from the safety behind the computers.

The posts have been so vile that Matejka has shut down his social media accounts, only to have conspiracy theorists calling the survivors "crisis actors" hired to pose as victims target his loved ones, instead.

"There are all these families dealing with likely the most horrific thing they'll ever experience, and they are also met with hate and anger and are being attacked online about being part of some conspiracy," his brother, Taylor Matejka, said in an interview with the Guardian. "It's madness I can't imagine the thought process of these people. Do they know that we are actual people?"

Braden Matejka had attended the concert with his girlfriend, Amanda Homulos, as a 30th birthday gift to himself.

After he was struck by a bullet, Homulos flagged down the car of another concertgoer, who took the couple to a nearby hospital.

"I'm just so grateful that we're still here, and I can't express how sorry I am for the people that didn't make it," Homulos said.

That car ride was one of the defining moments of one of the year's most horrific events.

"If there's a silver lining to this event, it's the humanity of the event," said one witness. "It's everyone helps everyone."

People who were running for their lives–"There's no reason why you wouldn't," said Heather Gooze–but instead of putting their own interests first, they stopped to help others, lifting them up off the bloodied ground, dragging them if they couldn't walk on their own, doing what comes naturally to wartime soldiers by making sure that no man or woman was left behind.

"We cannot let the actions of a single person define us as a country," said House speaker Paul Ryan (R-Wisconsin). "It's not who we are. Instead, what truly defines us are the acts of heroism we witness after the tragedy."

Las Vegas, circa 2014

The last time Las Vegas experienced such a random act of horrific violence was on June 8, 2014, when Jerad and Amanda Miller, a married couple with a vendetta against the government, went on a shooting spree, killing two Las Vegas police officers who were enjoying a quick lunch at CiCi's Pizza, then stole their guns and ammo and pinned a note to one of the officer's body that read, "This is the beginning of the revolution."

That revolution was short-lived, however.

The Millers' next stop was a nearby Walmart, where an armed civilian attempted to intervene before being shot himself.

Jerad Miller was killed by police soon after, and Amanda Miller took her own life after she was injured by police gunfire.

Just before the attack, Jerad Miller left the following post on Facebook: "The dawn of a new day. May all of our coming sacrifices be worth it."

October

TAMPA NEIGHBORHOOD ON EDGE OVER SERIAL KILLER CONCERNS

On October 9, college student Benjamin Mitchell, 22, was just hoping to catch a bus.

Mitchell was waiting for a Hillsborough Regional Transit Authority (HART) bus on North 15th Street at Frierson Avenue when he was fatally shot.

Witnesses told police they saw a man in his early 20s running from the area, wearing a dark, hooded jacket.

"I've come up with four reasons why this person is running," interim Tampa Police Chief Brian Dugan said. "One, they may be late for dinner. Two, they're out exercising. Three, they heard gunshots, and, number four, they just murdered Benjamin Mitchell."

In a video released by police, the person of interest, tall and slim, first is seen walking toward the bus stop where Mitchell was killed, then running away immediately afterwards.

Police were quick to say the person in the video is not necessarily a suspect, but could have information valuable to their case.

Dugan said the person might be easy to identify because they were seen casually flipping what appears to be a cellphone in their right hand while walking, which could be a habit that might make them memorable to somebody in the neighborhood.

"At this point, everything is a clue, everything is a speculation," Dugan said, adding that every bit of information should be seen as important.

According to Mitchell's aunt, Angie Dupree, he was at the bus stop in order to ensure his girlfriend made it home safely.

Mitchell was living in Tampa so he could grow up in a good environment, his aunt added, and was working at Ikea in order to pay for his classes at Hillsborough Community College.

"I can't believe that someone took my nephew for no good reason at all. You got away with nothing. You took a child's life for no reason at all, because you didn't get anything," she said.

Second murder was equally mysterious

Romano Whitley had just gotten home to her Seminole Heights neighborhood house on October 11 when she heard the pop of gunshots

She thought they were firecrackers, though, and when she looked out of her bedroom window and saw nothing and heard nothing more, she didn't think about the sounds again.

It wasn't until two days later, when Whitley made a call to the city to mow the grass on a nearby lot that the city owned, that she realized the horrible truth of what she had heard on October 11, two nights after Benjamin Mitchell was killed.

In the overgrown grass, city officials found sign language teacher Monica Hoffa, 32, dead of gunshot wounds.

"No one could see her in the grass," said Whitley. "It's very, very disturbing."

Hoffa was the second in a series of killings that police now believe are linked.

"In addition to the relatively close time frame, the proximity of the shootings, the nature of the two shootings, it has led our detectives to believe they are related," said Dugan. "These are people who aren't living a lifestyle that would lead to the fact they may end up getting murdered."

"It's just dangerous. It's dangerous to be out here," said one resident, wiping away tears. "You don't know who this guy is, and he's got a gun. His purpose is to just kill people, you know? They're not robbing anybody."

Third victim died after taking wrong bus

Anthony Naiboa, 20, was autistic, but that didn't stop him from living.

One of five siblings, he had just graduated from high school and worked packing hurricane relief supplies, according to his father, Casimar Naiboa.

But because his normal bus route home was shut down on October 19, he took a different route, and ended up in a neighborhood that was unfamiliar to the young man, who did best when following a routine.

"He wasn't any threat to nobody, he never did nothing to nobody," Casimar Naiboa said. "I can't believe my son is gone."

Naiboa died on the sidewalk near the home where the first victim, Benjamin Mitchell lived, and police heard the gunshots.

"He was in the prime of his life and was taken instantly," said Dugan. "Our officers heard the gunshots. We have a heavy presence, and this person was able to sneak away. I was convinced we were going to catch this person."

They did not, despite using a helicopter, a SWAT team and K9 units.

While police still didn't use the term "serial killer," they believe that the same person is responsible for all three shootings.

Despite that, police have no motives for the string of murders, since victims are only connected by the bus system.

Seminole Heights residents, however, are growing decidedly more nervous.

"It's bad when you hear about it elsewhere but seeing it in your own backyard, it strikes a little bit more of a chord closer to home," said Seminole Heights resident Rachael Laurent. "I don't necessarily feel comfortable out in the neighborhood late at night or even after it's gone dark, especially if I'm by myself."

Some residents are just staying in at night in an attempt to protect themselves.

"There's no rhyme or reason, so we all feel a little shaken and concerned that we could be the next victim," said Stan Lasater, president of the Southeast Seminole Heights Civic Association.

"We've always had small, petty crimes," Lasater said. "But when we had the first murder, the community was really shaken. And then we had the second, and third, and now the community is definitely on alert."

Fourth victim was caught by surprise

Ronald Felton, 60, was walking across the street in his Seminole Heights neighborhood when he was shot and killed just before 5 a.m. on November 19.

The fourth victim in a little more than a month, Felton was killed a few blocks away from a memorial that was set up to honor the first three victims, Mitchell, Hoffa and Naiboa.

According to witnesses, the suspect is a black man about 6' tall with a thin build and light complexion. He was dressed in dark clothing and was carrying a pistol.

Felton was out so early because he helped serve the homeless on Tuesdays and Fridays, and he was at the food pantry setting up. His bike was found outside the pantry.

His killing put the entire community on edge.

"We have someone who's terrorizing the neighborhood," said Dugan, who now firmly believes that the person in the surveillance video is their suspect, or at least knows something about the four crimes.

"Through the proximity, and the timeframe, they are related," Dugan said. "There is no doubt in our mind about that."

He told people to be vigilant, but to continue to live their lives as usual.

"We're not going to be held hostage," he said.

Public likely has answers

Romano Whitley had been up at night, spending the hours staring out the window where Hoffa's body was found.

Lasater, meanwhile, said that the association is promoting a porch light campaign to make it more difficult for the suspect to travel through Seminole Heights without being spotted.

"We're making it harder for this guy to sneak about the neighborhood unseen," he said.

People in the neighborhood have held marches and vigils, and candles burn at the locations where the victims' bodies were found.

Police, meanwhile, are reviewing "extensive amount of video" from the HART bus system's surveillance cameras in hopes of catching a glimpse of one person at the bus stop closest to each crime scene, an extensive, arduous task.

According to HART spokesperson Sandra Morrison, the transit agency has been working extensively with the Tampa police department since the start of the investigation.

"We have shared an extensive amount of video clips," she said, including clips from Route 9, the bus that services the Seminole Heights area where the shootings occurred.

Meanwhile, to protect passengers and perhaps throw off the perpetrator, HART is rerouting route 9, making it more difficult for the shooter to target victims on that route.

A reward of more than $100,000 has been offered for information to help solve the case.

"We still have no leads, we still have no motives, but it's clear to me that these are all linked. I want people to look at the video. I want people to see how this person walks," Dugan said. "We don't need speculation, we don't need profiles, we just need names."

People living their lives normally will also help protect the neighborhood.

"They're by themselves. This person is working under the cover of darkness," Dugan said. "The more people that are outside, the more people that are in the neighborhood, frequenting the businesses, that's what's going to help put a stop to this."

"We will hunt this person down until we find them," added Tampa Mayor Bob Buckhorn. "Nobody comes into our house and does this. This is your community and we are not going to let evil win this race."

What kind of person might be behind the murders?

According to profiler Enzo Yaksic, who operates the Serial Homicide Expertise and Information Sharing Collaborative, a database of thousands of murders, if the persona responsible for the four shootings is the same, there are some clues being left behind with each crime.

"It is likely that the offender maintains a deep and personal relationship with the area, residing within a few blocks of the crime scenes and arriving to each location on foot or via bicycle," Yaksic wrote in a profile he shared with Tampa's News Channel 8.

He believes that whoever committed the murders is in his or her 20s or 30s, suggesting "gangland activity and initiation rituals."

Yaksic said he believes that the killer is likely a minority, and "the disparity between the offender's perceived lower status may be driving his motivations to victimize those from other statuses."

He continued by suggesting that the killer is not living a traditional life, although he may have a day job due to the times when the crimes are carried out.

"The victimization of others while they are completing everyday tasks, while not the offender's primary motivation, rounds out a profile of an individual with a disdain for constructs such as wealth and stature oftentimes flouted by today's society," Yaksic wrote.

Yaksic suggested looking back at shootings over the last six months to see if any could be related to the recent rash of murders, which suggest escalation on the part of the suspect, since so many were occurring in such a short span of time.

Man arrested in shootings

It turns out Yaksic was pretty dead-on in his profile of the shooter terrorizing Seminole Heights.

On November 28, a worker at a local McDonald's was arrested for the shootings after bringing a loaded handgun into his place of employment.

Howell Emanuel Donaldson III, 24, will be charged with four counts of first-degree murder.

Police were tipped off to Donaldson, a black man who fits both the minority and economic status categories of Yaksic's profile, when he left his loaded 9mm handgun with a co-worker while he went to a nearby payday loan establishment for some quick cash, according to the Tampa Bay Times.

Donaldson was arrested after he returned to his place of work, where police were waiting.

Although they declined to release details about the arrest, it's likely police were able to match the gun to the weapon used in the four shootings based on ballistics testing as well as other information.

"Things are starting to fall into place," said Dugan. "But we've had that before and unfortunately, it's led to nothing. I'm guarded because I've been on this road before. It's day 51 that we've been doing this. It's been two weeks since Ronald Felton was murdered. It's been a long time for the families and the cops, and so I'm guarded on the whole thing, but I'm very optimistic. This will be a long night."

According to Dugan, Tampa police have received more than 5,000 tips since the murders began in early October.

"I am nervous, and I really, I want this to be the end of this," said Monica Hoffa's father, Kenny Hoffa. "It is like riding a roller coaster right before you go over the edge and you feel your stomach raise up in your face. This is the same thing. I am just extremely optimistic myself. I am praying that this is the end to it."

Tampa Mayor Bob Buckhorn also spoke at the press conference.

"Tonight, goodness has won," Buckhorn said. "Tonight, in the battle between darkness and light, light has won."

Donaldson is currently being held by the Hillsborough County Department of Detention Services.

Man kills, dismembers wife while children watch

A homeless Kansas City man is charged with abandoning a corpse after his wife's dismembered body was found in a cooler at a storage facility a week before Halloween.

Justin Rey, 35, had already been arrested and charged with child endangerment after he and his children, a two-year-old girl and an infant girl, were found in a storage unit at the U-Haul storage facility in Lenexa, Kansas, about 15 miles away from the hotel room where Rey and his wife had been living since September 25.

According to police, when Rey and the children were found, the baby wasn't wearing adequate clothing to protect her from the elements, and she was suffering from an eye infection.

Police had been tipped off about Rey after being contacted by workers at the storage facility, who said the suspicious man was talking about his wife dying while giving birth.

After Rey was arrested for child endangerment, police asked him where his wife was. He told them that she had died several days earlier from suicide after giving birth and could be found in the cooler and one of the totes that he had been attempting to remove from the storage unit.

According to Rey, his wife, Jessica Monteiro Rey, 32, had given birth on October 20. He then told authorities the two different stories–first, that his wife had died during childbirth in the hotel room, then, that she had committed suicide due to post-partum depression shortly after giving birth.

Her remains were discovered stuffed in the cooler and a plastic tote, just as Rey said they would.

Family was hiding from social services

According to Sara Monteiro, her sister gave birth in the hotel room rather than a hospital because they were attempting to hide their children from authorities.

The birth of the two-year-old girl had also been concealed, Sara said, because the couple's four older children had previously been taken into custody of Child Protective Services, through which at least two of them had been legally adopted.

And even if Rey didn't kill his wife, Sara still holds him responsible for her sister's death.

"He's 100 percent responsible. He's not admitting he killed her, he's not saying he didn't," she said.

Because she needed medical help when giving birth and he didn't get it for her, he is at fault, she said. "He neglected her chance of survival."

Rey was controlling and abusive

According to Sara, who hadn't seen her sister's face in more than a decade, Jessica graduated from high school with plans to be a fashion designer, and had a creative, artistic style that made her stand out from the others.

But then she met Rey, and "she fell head over heels in love with him," Sara said. They married in 2004, and a cycle of abuse that Jessica had known as a child continued into her marriage.

"That's what my sister knew as love, and that's what she married," Sara said.

Last days in hotel were morbid ones

Rey apparently was controlling to the end.

After he was arrested, he told police that he and the kids had spent two days sharing a room with his wife's corpse after she died. And after posing for pictures with the children and her dead body, he dismembered his wife in the hotel room bathtub where she'd also given birth.

He stuffed what he could into a cooler and a tote, then boiled some of the remains on a stove and flushed the rest down the hotel room toilet.

Inside the hotel room, the bathtub's drain had been removed, and human tissue and traces of blood were found throughout the room.

According to hotel staff, when Rey called the front desk to check out on October 23, he attempted to disguise his voice to sound female in an effort to throw staff off and make them believe that his wife was still alive.

He forgot about the surveillance video.

On the tapes, he is shown pulling a red cooler with a black bag on top while pushing a stroller as a toddler walked beside him. His wife was nowhere to be seen.

He apparently got a ride to the storage facility from a couple who took pity on the single man walking along the street with two young children and so much heavy luggage.

Sisters say police identified Jessica Monteiro Rey's remains

It had been a year since Rhonda Monteiro and Sara Monteiro had seen their sister, and now, all they will have is memories.

"All I have is the good memories. Us playing as kids and us growing up together," Rhonda Monteiro said in an interview, adding that she will sorely miss what the future might have held for the siblings.

According to the sisters, Rey's controlling nature kept the women apart and led them to miss getting to know their nieces, including the newborn who was just five days old when she was found in the same storage unit with her sister and father.

"The minute he got in her life, I never saw her again," Rhonda said, adding that her sister's grisly death was much too soon.

The sisters learned last week that Monteiro Rey's dismembered remains were found in a cooler inside a storage unit when they got a call from police.

"They told me he cut her up and put her in the ice chest," Sara said. "They said they weren't even able to identify whether it was male or female it was so bad. When I saw it on the news before anything was determined, I knew it was her because of our history with Justin."

Since the wedding, Rey and Jessica had moved from state to state, so the sisters weren't even certain where her sister was when she died.

"I can't even process it. We don't even get to see her, mourn her, see her and say goodbye. He took that away from us," Rhonda said.

The children are currently in protective custody until Monteiro Rey's family can determine appropriate arrangements for the girls.

Rey will undergo psychological evaluation

Rey's attorney, Courtney Henderson, made a motion in Johnson County Court requesting a psychological evaluation for his client, saying he has "good faith belief" that Rey is not capable of understanding the charges against him.

Rey, Henderson said, is not able to "effectively assist in his defense due to a mental or physical condition," based on their discussions regarding his case.

A judge granted the motion to assess Rey's ability to assist in his defense. The evaluation will be conducted at the Johnson County Mental Health Center.

Rey a suspect in California murder

On November 23, Justin Tod Rey was charged in the murder of Sean Ty Ferel, who went missing in May of 2016.

The Palm Springs, California, man was vacationing with Rey when he vanished. Three months later, Rey crashed Ferel's vehicle in an accident in Los Angeles.

Although Ferel's body has yet to be located, his blood was found in the trunk of his car Rey was driving and his possessions were found in an Arizona storage unit rented by Rey.

Rey is currently being held in Kansas on a $1 million bond, facing child endangerment charges. He is also charged with abandonment of a corpse in Missouri, where his wife died.

A serial killer may have been captured in Japan in similar dismemberment case

A week after Jessica Rey's body was discovered in Kansas City, Halloween came with real-life horrors in Tokyo, Japan, when investigators discovered the dismembered remains for nine bodies in an apartment of a 27-year-old man.

The case was reminiscent of German cannibal Armin Meiwes, who killed and then consumed 43-year-old computer technician Bernd Brandes in 2001. According to Meiwes, Brandes went willingly to his death, which is similar to the story 27-year-old Takahiro Shiraishi told police when they came to his apartment in search of a missing 24-year-old woman.

The woman had posted on a suicidal ideation site searching for someone to join her in a suicide pact, and Shiraishi apparently accepted her request, even though he himself had no intention of dying.

"There is no doubt that I tried to hide the body of the person I killed," said Takahiro Shiraishi, who confessed to killing one person, dismembering the body, and mixing the remains with cat litter before storing the morbid mixture in coolers. "I dismembered it at the bathroom, disposing of some body parts in the garbage."

Unfortunately for Shiraishi, his story fell apart when police found two severed heads in one cooler and the remains of nine bodies, including eight women and one man, amid the cat litter mixture in other coolers, creating a stench in his apartment so foul that it caused neighbors to recoil in horror.

Shiraishi, who also had a saw that officials believed he used to dismember the bodies, was arrested, and is being held on suspicions of being a serial killer.

WOMAN CHARGED WITH MURDER WARNED AGAINST FORCED MARRIAGE

When a woman doesn't want to get married, sometimes it's best not to push the issue.

In Pakistan, almost 20 people would still be alive if the husband of Aasia Bibi had stopped proposing after she refused a second time, and if her parents had listened to their 21-year-old daughter when she told them she would do anything to get out of a marriage they finally arranged for her after she refused the man a third time.

It took about a month for the Pakistani woman in love with someone else to go through with plans to end her arranged marriage. A union she had protested until she and a man she did not love met at the altar in a village near the town of Ali Pur, 60 miles south of Multan.

The two families were not only neighbors on the same street in the small village of Malawat, but they were also related, which made the parents feel secure in the union, despite how unwelcome it was to the daughter.

"Arranged marriage is a source of comfort for most parents here as they feel that the existing close ties between families will strengthen the new relationship, said Pakistani official Salman Sufi in the New York Times.

For younger people, however, the tradition is one that is no longer welcome, as many young people are forming their own romantic relationships with people they truly love.

"The result often is a severely fractured relationship between spouses or catastrophic aftereffects, like we witnessed in this case," Sufi said.

Unhappiness in the marriage is even worse, according to National

Public Radio's Diaa Hadid.

"In Pakistan, marriages arranged by families with minimal input by the bride and groom are common, although that is changing in urban areas. But in particularly traditional families, daughters are expected to comply entirely with their parent's wishes," she said.

Girls are often promised to relatives or wealthier men when they are quite young, and divorce is not seen as an option, as it would bring shame upon the family while pushing it into deep debt. Because of these personal burdens, women often stay in unhappy or violent marriages, Hadid added.

"But cases such as this—where a woman tries to kill her husband— is unusual. In Pakistan it is often the other way around: the country is one of the most dangerous in the world to be female," Hadid reported.

Wife had repeatedly protested union

"I repeatedly asked my parents not to marry me against my will as my religion, Islam, also allows me to choose the man of my choice for marriage but my parents rejected all of my pleas and they married me to a relative," said Aasia Bibi, who was seeing a boyfriend, Muhammad Shahid Lashari, and continued seeing him after the arranged marriage vows were exchanged in September.

But Bibi had told her family that she would do anything to get out of the arranged marriage with her cousin–a common practice in Pakistan–and the lengths to which she would go apparently even meant murder.

Unfortunately for her, her plans to rid herself of her husband with poisoned milk initially failed, and she accidentally killed seventeen other people with the milk meant for the husband she detested.

Murder could have been avoided

Days before the unfortunate incident, Bibi fled the home she'd briefly shared with her cousin and sought refuge with her parents, but they were not sympathetic to her plight, even though she begged them to let her stay.

According to National Public Radio, Bibi's parents again forced her to do something against her will, this time to return to the home she shared with the husband she hated.

Trapped, she was now more desperate than ever.

The woman said she asked Lashari for rat poison, and he obliged, giving her the deadly substance that she mixed in her husband's milk, but he did not drink it. Instead, the glass of milk sat in Bibi's refrigerator for a week before her mother-in-law spotted it and mixed the milk in the traditional yogurt-based drink called a lassi, which she then served to 27 people.

(A lassi is a blend of yogurt, water, spices and sometimes fruit. It can be savory, with roasted cumin, or sweet, seasoned with sugar.)

Authorities said 17 people died, including Bibi's husband, Muhammad Amjad, and 10 were hospitalized after drinking the lassi.

Bibi drew suspicions

According to local police chief Zulfiqar Ali, Bibi drew suspicion almost immediately, especially because she was the only person who did not drink the lassi, but also due to her behavior at the hospital.

"Her husband was in critical condition at a hospital, and she looked as if nothing had happened and she was cool and calm at her home and it raised suspicions," he said.

Bibi was remorseful over the deaths and told police her husband was her only target.

They had been married for just six months, "but she was not happy

218

with the marriage," officials said, adding that the relationship between the two was severely strained.

Police sought to determine who was the real killer

According to district police chief Sohail Habib Tajek, police spent two weeks questioning Bibi to determine whether or not it was her decision or that of her boyfriend to poison her husband.

"This incident took place last week, and our officers have made progress by arresting a woman and her lover in connection with this murder case, which was complicated and challenging for us," he said in an interview with The Associated Press.

In the early days of questioning, Bibi told police a poison lizard must have fallen into the milk, but soon realized that story was not going to work on officials, and then she confessed.

In addition to Bibi and her lover Shahid Lashari, who was also arrested and charged with murder, Bibi's aunt, 49-year-old Zarina Begum, who had allowed the two to meet at her home, was also arrested because she was aware of the plot to kill Bibi's husband.

Village elder Abdul Majid said that if the opportunity presented itself, he would behead Bibi and her boyfriend to restore honor to the village, now under international scrutiny.

"If I see them, I will behead them with a wood saw," he said.

After her daughter's arrest, Bibi's mother, Zakia Begum, expressed regret for forcing her daughter to marry a man she detested.

"I feel guilty and I think we should have not forced our daughter to marry Amjad, as she did not like him," she told The Associated Press.

TERRORIST RENTS TRUCK, MOWS DOWN BICYCLISTS IN NYC

At about 2 p.m. on October 31, 29-year-old Sayfullo Saipov rented a truck from Home Depot in New Jersey.

An hour later, a few blocks from the New York Trade Center, in the shadow of the site where the deadliest terror attack in U.S. history took place, he took a wrong turn, driving down a bike path, killing at least eight people and injuring several others before slamming into a school bus, injuring four more people–two adults and two children.

By 3:08 p.m. New York City officials were fielding numerous 911 calls reporting the incident.

After his path of devastation, he got out of the truck wielding a fake gun in each hand, yelling "Allahu Akbar," ("God is great" in Arabic) before police shot him in the abdomen.

"This was an act of terror," New York Mayor Bill de Blasio declared at an evening press conference. "A particularly cowardly act of terror aimed at innocent civilians, aimed at innocent people going about their lives."

Scene was chaos

"The Home Depot truck started running people over," said witness Nelson Arroyo, 58. "I heard a boom, a crushing noise from the bikes. People were sitting down crying. I saw two areas of blood."

After driving nearly a mile down a bike path filled with people enjoying a leisurely cruise along the Hudson River, Saipov collided with a school bus at Chambers Street, injuring two adults and two children inside.

The crash, however, crumpled his front end and put the rental truck–

and his terror attack–out of commission.

Tom Gay, a school photographer, heard that there had been an accident, and he walked down to West Street, when a woman came screaming around the corner, "He has a gun! He has a gun!"

That's when Gay peeked around the corner, spotting a slender man in a blue tracksuit running down West Street, a gun in each hand.

He was being chased by a cop who might have been heavyset, but knew his way around a foot chase.

The officer, later identified as NYPD's Ryan Nash, shot the man in the tracksuit–Gay said he heard five or six shots–who turned out to be Saipov, an immigrant from Uzbekistan who had legally entered the United States in 2010 and was carrying a Florida driver's license.

Nash then walked over and kicked the gun, which turned out to be nothing but an air gun, out of the terrorist's hand.

The officer was also injured and transported to a local hospital, according to NYPD Commissioner James O'Neill.

The bodies of those who had not survived the attack were covered with white sheets and remained on the path, the crumpled remains of their rental bikes nearby.

"I saw a lot of blood over there. A lot of people on the ground," said Chen Yi, an Uber driver who was in the area when the attack occurred.

Eugene Duffy, a chef at a waterfront restaurant, said police sirens and screams soon masked any other sounds.

Nash hailed a hero

Ryan Nash, 28, is a decorated, five-year veteran of the NYPD stationed in Lower Manhattan.

And after his shooting of the terror suspect, he was praised by officials throughout the city and state.

"He was a hero," Gov. Andrew Cuomo said. "I think Officer Nash showed how important (patrol officers) are, and how talented they are and how brave. So, we all applaud and congratulate him."

Nash and another officer were responding to an unrelated call Tuesday afternoon at Stuyvesant High School when they were alerted by civilians about an apparent car crash nearby, said John Miller, NYPD deputy commissioner.

When they arrived at the scene, they encountered a man waving guns in the air, bodies around him.

It had to be a horrifyingly vivid moment to take in, but Nash was undeterred by the nightmare of it all, and he chased the man until he was close enough to fire his weapon.

Police Commissioner James P. O'Neill said the weapons Saipov was carrying were later determined to be a paintball gun and a pellet gun. But there was no way for Nash to know that when he confronted the suspect, O'Neill said.

"This is what he did for the city, and this is what he did for the country," O'Neill said. "I'm really proud of him."

Ryan was briefly hospitalized for minor injuries and released.

Nash, a native of New Jersey, lives on Long Island with his girlfriend.

"Here's the hero cop the world should be talking about," City Councilman Joe Borelli said in a tweet that included Nash's photo. "Police Officer Ryan Nash risked his life to save others. Thank u Ryan, thank u #NYPD."

Who is Sayfullo Saipov?

Sayfullo Saipov rented a truck from the town where he lived, Paterson, New Jersey–home to the second-largest Muslim population in the United States by percentage–a week before the terror attack so he would have a chance to learn how to drive the vehicle.

Thankfully, he didn't learn very well, as he had planned to continue on to the Brooklyn Bridge for more carnage but instead crashed with the school bus, ultimately saving more lives.

Police say he has no remorse for what he did. In fact, he said he is "proud" to have killed eight people, which is in line with radical Islamic beliefs.

He had planned to display ISIS flags on the front and back of the truck during his attack but thought better of it because he did not want to draw too much attention to himself.

Saipov apparently had been planning his attack for several weeks, according to police investigations, although he had never been under the watch of either the FBI or NYPD, suggesting that he was not a key member of ISIS until the attack in Manhattan.

Experts said that Saipov followed the instructions ISIS posts on its social media channels on how to carry out such an attack, "almost to a T," according to John Miller, New York Police Department deputy commissioner for intelligence and counter-terrorism

Police found multiple knives in Saipov's vehicle, and countless videos and photos related to ISIS on his cell phone, including 90 videos and 3,800 images, including photos of ISIS prisoners being beheaded, run over with tanks, or shot to death.

On Twitter, President Donald Trump referred to Saipov as a "very sick and deranged person" and said that he "SHOULD GET THE DEATH PENALTY!"

Saipov first lived in Ohio, where he married Nozima Odilova in Cuyahoga Falls in 2013, when he was 25 and she was 19, then later lived in Fort Myers, Florida. In both places, he earned a living as a truck driver, but moved to New Jersey to work as an Uber driver. He passed his Uber background check.

A friend called him "a very good guy," although he admitted he didn't know everything about Saipov, who apparently kept some very dark secrets.

Prior to the attack, his criminal record only included traffic offenses, which were incurred in Missouri and Iowa.

When contacted by authorities, his mother-in-law, who lives in Brooklyn, said she was in shock over the incident.

"I don't know what happened," she said.

The victims

Most of the victims were tourists, so the attack reached around the world, touching lives in Europe, South America, and the United States.

Those dead include:

- Nicholas Cleves, 24. A web developer with extreme promise, Cleves was a graduate from Skidmore College who worked at Unified Digital, a software company owned by Alex Silverstein, who said Cleves was gifted with even the most frustrating customer, and had dreams of a bold future. "It's about the promise," Silverstein said. "He is like the future of programming and software, and now he's gone." Cleves also designed the website for his parents' SoHo handblown glass company, CX design, owned by Richard Cleves and Monica Missio.

- Hernán Mendoza, Diego Angelini, Alejandro Pagnucco, Ariel Erlij, and Hernán Ferruchi. The Argentinians were celebrating their 30th class reunion with a trip to New York City. They had graduated from the Instituto Politécnico Superior in Rosario, a city north of Buenos Aires. In a photograph taken at the airport, they all wore T-shirts that read "Libre" ("Free" in

English), and seemed excited about their adventure. Erlij, who owned a steel mill, had paid the fares for some of his 1987 classmates to accompany them on the trip.

- Ann-Laure Decadt, 31. Decadt, of Belgium, had come to New York with her mother and two sisters. Her husband, Alexander Naessens, received a call from New York-Presbyterian Hospital less than an hour after the attack that killed his wife, who was riding a bicycle along the Hudson River with her family when she was hit by the rental truck. "This loss is unbearable and incomprehensible," he said. She was "a fantastic wife and the most wonderful mother of our two little sons of 3 months and 3 years old. It's hard to imagine that someone who goes on a holiday can be taken out of life so brutally."

- Darren Drake, 32. The morgue where Drake's parents went to identify his body was three blocks from the hospital where his son was born. "Looking at your son in a morgue, with the scars and black and blue," Jimmy Drake said, "I didn't see my son of 32 years of age. I saw a newborn." Drake worked as a project manager for Moody's Analytics and spent his work breaks riding his bike along the Hudson River.

New York governor Andrew Cuomo echoed the words of a nation when he spoke at a press conference following the event.

"Our thoughts and prayers are with those New Yorkers who we lost today—it reminds us all how precious life is," Cuomo said. "They left the house this morning—they were enjoying the beautiful West Side of Manhattan on a beautiful fall day and they are not going to be returning home. And that shock and that pain is going to be very real."

"We know that this action was intended to break our spirit, but we also know New Yorkers are strong, New Yorkers are resilient," de Blasio added. "And our spirit will never be moved by an act of violence, an act meant to intimidate us."

225

Aftermath

On November 21, a federal grand jury handed down a 22-count indictment against Sayfullo Saipov for his role in the Manhattan terror attack.

His charges range from terrorism to both murder and attempted murder in aid of racketeering in connection to the October 31 terror attack, which left eight people dead and twelve wounded.

The murder in aid of racketeering charge is generally used by federal prosecutors in organized crime cases.

"Consumed by hate and a twisted ideology, Sayfullo Saipov allegedly barreled down a pedestrian walkway and bicycle path on a sunny afternoon on the west side of Manhattan, killing eight innocent people," acting U.S. Attorney Joon Kim said.

Saipov has been in federal custody since the attack.

His charges make him eligible for the death penalty.

According to police, Saipov asked to display ISIS's flag in his hospital room and felt no remorse–actually stated that he felt good–about what he had done.

November

MOM SHOOTS TWO DAUGHTERS, THEN CONFESSES TO HUSBAND

"My wife just shot her kids," said an anguished Jacob Henderson in a 911 call, seconds after his wife attempted to shoot him as well, only to have the gun malfunction.

It was just two hours after police responded to an earlier 911 call at the home, when Henderson called and said his wife, Sarah Nicole Henderson, 29, was behaving strangely.

"I want to get somebody out here to check my wife out," Jacob Henderson said, telling the dispatcher that he didn't think his wife was suicidal, but she was "freaking out like someone is out to get her."

Seven minutes later, Henderson called again. His wife was now okay and he wanted to cancel his earlier request for help.

Despite the request, Deputies arrived at the family's home in Mabank, Texas–about 55 miles southeast of Dallas–15 minutes after the call, which had come in at 11:29 p.m. Wednesday.

When they arrived, the couple refused help.

Officers apparently spoke with both of them, according to Sheriff Bodie Hillhouse, and were told that all was well in the home, so deputies left, assuming everything was fine in the Henderson house.

Jacob Henderson then fell asleep.

When he awoke, it was to these horrifying words from his wife: "Jake, I shot the kids."

When he checked in disbelief, he saw that yes, both girls had been shot in the head, and both girls were dead, their long blond hair now drenched in blood.

Again, he called 911, this time not even capable of being calm.

Second call is much different

Three hours after making that first call, at 2:24 a.m. Thursday, Jacob Henderson was struggling to keep hold of the gun he'd taken from his wife while telling the 911 dispatcher that his stepdaughters, 7-year-old Kaylee Hall and 5-year-old Kenlie Pallett, were dead.

"She was asleep when I went to sleep last night. I woke up and she came in there said, 'Babe, I just shot the kids.' And I didn't want to believe it. I went in there, and they were dead," Henderson said.

As he speaks to the 911 dispatcher, Sarah seems to not understand, and says, "What's going on here Jake?"

Her husband replied, "Nothing's going on! That's what I tried telling you! She keeps saying somebody is after her. There's nobody after her. She keeps saying people are coming—there's nobody even here."

He then told the dispatcher that the girls had been asleep in the living room when their mother shot them, and that he could see the blood from the gunshot wounds they had sustained to their heads.

In the background, Sarah Henderson could then be heard asking, "Why did I do that, Jake?" while Jacob himself asked the same question, repeating, "Why?" over and over.

Sarah Henderson only replied, "I'm sorry," before begging her husband to shoot her rather than allow her to face the consequences of what she had done. He told her he couldn't do it, the 911 dispatcher listening all the while.

Hendersons hadn't been married long

The Hendersons were still newlyweds and had only been together a few years based on photos of the girls from their wedding, many used in news stories about their horrifying murders.

As attendants, Kaylee and Kenlie had worn denim shirts, white tutus, and cowboy boots at the wedding, along with floral headbands and big smiles.

They appeared to be the happiest of families, but sometimes, looks can be very, very deceiving.

Sarah Henderson has another child, a son, Wyatt, who lives with his father outside the county.

Murder leaves neighbors saddened, shocked

In the days following the murders, neighbors questioned what had been going on in the yellow single-wide trailer that still had its Halloween decorations up a week after the holiday was over.

"You don't ever know who you're living across the street from," says Jaylyne Palmer, a neighbor of the family. "So, you would never think of something like this happening."

Still, Palmer didn't get a lot of warm fuzzies from the woman who lived across the street, with whom she never shared a conversation but would recognize the woman's voice all the same, because she heard her yelling at the girls often, using terrible language and speaking loudly enough that it was not just for the family's ears.

"You could hear her all over the neighborhood yelling," Palmer said. "I felt sorry for the kids but I didn't think she did anything to them. Evidently, I guess I was wrong."

The girls, however, were sweet neighbors who rode their bikes–training wheels still attached–through the trailer park and drew pictures for the Palmers, leaving them in the mailbox for the family.

"They were so sweet, it's just hard," Palmer said. "We'll miss the little girls."

Police, social services had previously visited Henderson's home

According to Sheriff Bodie Hillhouse, police had been dispatched to the house once before in 2015 for what was called a "verbal disturbance."

What they encountered was Sarah Henderson, standing in her yard, having an argument with someone over her cell phone.

Texas Child Protective Services had also been in contact with the family in 2010, before Jake and Sarah were married, but the details of that investigation are confidential.

Both girls attended Southside Elementary in Mabank, and both students and staff were understandably devastated by the news of the girls' deaths.

Counselors were on hand to help students, faculty members, and parents cope with the loss.

Henderson had planned murders

According to Sarah Henderson, she had been planning to murder her young daughters as well as her husband for more than two weeks before she pulled off at least part of her crime. She had also planned to kill herself.

"She did try to shoot her husband. The gun malfunctioned. He took the pistol and then realized the daughters had been shot," Hillhouse said. "We don't have a motive at all. We're still digging, trying to figure out what was going on at that house at the time."

"She was very matter of fact, to the point, and just didn't show any remorse," Hillhouse said. "The only thing she told us was that she had smoked some marijuana early in the evening. She was very

230

blunt. We just don't have any answers as to why."

Mental health apparently played a role.

Sarah Henderson's mother, Teresa Brown, told NBC that she has bipolar disorder and that she had been having trouble dealing with her disorder in recent weeks.

"Something snapped in her, because she loved her kids," Brown said in the interview. "I'm just devastated. The whole family is. We're just zombies, it's just unbelievable."

Crime echoes a similar shooting a year earlier

In June of 2016, Christy Sheats killed her two daughters, Taylor, 22, and Madison, 17, to punish her husband because the couple decided to get a divorce.

Jason Sheats said that Christy "wanted him to suffer" when she killed the two girls during a family meeting in the living room of their Texas home.

Jason Sheats told police that Christy killed the girls because she knew not only how much he loved Taylor and Madison, but also how much they loved him, Fort Bend County Sheriff Troy E. Nehls said during a press conference following the shooting.

Christy Sheats, who refused to drop her gun after the family fled outside the home, was shot and killed by a Fulshear police officer.

For Jason Sheats, his once-happy life was forever destroyed.

"This is something he is going to have to live with for the rest of his life," Nehls said. "She accomplished what she set out to do, which is to make him suffer."

TEXAS CHURCH DEVASTATED BY WORST SHOOTING IN STATE HISTORY

The worst shooting death in Texas history should never have happened.

When 26-year-old Devin Patrick Kelley–an increasingly angry man who had been showing signs of a meltdown for years–opened fire on the church congregation at First Baptist Church in Sutherland Springs, Texas, about 40 miles southeast of San Antonio, killing 26 people including an unborn child, all vulnerably seated in church pews to pray, it was with a weapon that he should not have owned.

Kelley had been discharged from the military after he was court-martialed over a 2010 assault on his first wife and stepson, an incident that left the boy with a fractured skull and included pointing a loaded gun at his wife before beating and choking her.

It should have stopped him from obtaining a gun.

Still, he had purchased several weapons, including a Ruger semi-automatic rifle that is believed to be the gun he used when he left behind blood and carnage at the close-knit Texas church.

A nightmare for a congregation

It was almost half past 11 a.m. on Sunday, November 5, when Kelley, wearing black tactical gear and carrying a Ruger assault rifle, parked at a gas station across from First Baptist Church, crossed the street, and began shooting at the church.

According to survivors, he shouted, "Everybody fucking dies" when he entered the church, just before he began taking aim at parishioners.

Lorenzo Flores was at the gas station where Kelley had parked when he heard the shooting start.

232

"It sounded like he didn't want to take his finger off the trigger," Flores said. "It was nonstop."

Flores described the sound, a steady buzzing of bullets that suggested round after round after round of ammunition was being fired.

According to Roseanne Solis, who was inside the church with about 50 other people, he was looking around the church, quickly scanning the setting, and shooting at everyone that he saw.

The small church was targeted because it was attended by Kelley's wife's family, including her parents and grandmother. While authorities have not yet divulged what kind of beef Kelley had with his wife's family, it was enough to send him into a murderous rage.

Earlier that Sunday, before going to her house of worship, he had sent several threatening text messages to his mother-in-law, Michelle Shields, according to investigators.

She and her husband were not in church that day, but his ex-wife's grandmother was killed in the shooting, in which most people died attempting to protect loved ones from the onslaught of bullets filling the small house of worship.

The event devastated the tiny town of 400, and First Baptist's tight-knit congregation.

"I just cannot fathom why someone would do this," said First Baptist Church member Helen Biesenbach. "He killed all these innocent people and their little children, all for nothing. A madman."

Once inside, he targeted children

Solis and her husband, Joaquin Ramirez, thought they were hearing firecrackers at first, when Kelley started shooting outside the wood-frame church.

Soon, though, she watched other members of the congregation begin screaming and dropping to the ground as bullets bounced off the carpet and blood began spurting from countless bullet wounds.

The first to die were those taking photos and video of the service. After that, the associate pastor–on his way to the altar to conduct services for the church's pastor, who was out of town–was targeted.

There was a brief pause, perhaps as Kelley looked around and assessed the situation, before the shooting resumed. Kelley made his way up and down the aisles, Solis said, and seemed to specifically target children who were crying as the church filled with the acrid scent of gunfire.

"You've got your pews on either side. He just walked down the center aisle, turned around, and my understanding was shooting on his way back out," said Wilson County Sheriff Joe D. Tackitt Jr., who said that there was no available escape route for parishioners once the shooting began.

Both Solis and Ramirez were hit, but they survived by playing dead.

One of those killed was Annabelle Pomeroy, 14, the daughter of the church's pastor, Frank Pomeroy.

"Our church was not comprised of members or parishioners. We were a very close family," said Sherri Pomeroy, who was also out of town with her husband the day of the shooting. "Now most of our church family is gone."

The victims ranged in age from 18 months to 72 years. Many died in a desperate attempt to protect loved ones from Kelley's bullets.

The event caused federal law enforcement including investigators from the Federal Bureau of Alcohol, Tobacco, and Firearms, and members of the FBI to flood the rural community, a small town where everyone knew everyone, and almost every household knew someone who had been killed or injured.

"This is horrific for our tiny little tight-knit town," said Alena

Berlanga. "Everybody's going to be affected, and everybody knows someone who's affected."

Elected officials spoke during a news conference the next day.

"There are no words to describe the pure evil that we witnessed in Sutherland Springs today," said Texas Governor Greg Abbott at a news conference the day after the event. "Our hearts are heavy at the anguish in this small town, but in time of tragedy, we see the very best of Texas. May God comfort those who've lost a loved one, and may God heal the hurt in our communities."

Still, there were questions.

Why did Kelley have weapons?

Kelley clearly loved guns. He posted a tribute to his AR-15 semiautomatic weapon on social media, captioned, "She's a bad bitch."

But Kelley was not legally allowed to own any weapons.

The U.S. Air Force vet had worked in logistics readiness at Holloman Air Force Base in New Mexico from 2010 until 2014. He had been discharged for the assault on his previous wife and her child, which resulted in a court-martial as well as a 12-month stay in a military mental health facility.

According to his ex-wife, Tessa Brennaman, who filed for divorce shortly after the injury to her child, Kelley "had a lot of demons or hatred inside of him," including a hair-trigger temper.

After Brennaman had gotten a traffic ticket for speeding, Kelley threatened to kill her. Unfortunately, it was not the only time he threatened death to his young wife.

"He had a gun in his holster right here, and he took that gun out and he put it to my temple and he told me, 'Do you want to die? Do you want to die?'"

The marriage ended in 2012, when Kelley admitted hitting, choking, and kicking Brennaman and fracturing the skull of her young son.

Those charges should have legally prohibited Kelley from purchasing a gun, but the U.S. Air Force, in which Kelley had been an airman before receiving a "bad conduct" discharge, had failed to enter his information into the background check database, so when he lied on his application, he was approved for a gun permit.

"Somebody really dropped the ball," former Air Force chief prosecutor Col. Don Christensen told CNN.

If civilian law enforcement had been made aware of Kelley's court-martial, especially the reasons behind it, that information would have appeared in three separate databases that would have prevented Kelley from obtaining weapons, and he would have been denied the ability to purchase a gun.

In all, Kelley bought four weapons despite his negative military background, two in Colorado and two in Texas, according to the ATF.

Firearms charges dropped after plea

According to his military records, Kelley initially faced charges of assault and battery against his spouse, aggravated assault against his stepson, and four charges involving firearms, including two of pointing a loaded firearm at his wife and two of pointing an unloaded firearm.

Before his discharge, Kelley had also attempted to sneak firearms onto Holloman Air Force Base in New Mexico, after he had made death threats toward a superior officer.

In exchange for a guilty plea from Kelley, however, military prosecutors dropped the firearms charges, allowing Kelley to plead guilty to charges of aggravated assault against the child–he admitted to shaking and hitting his stepson with a force likely to produce death or grievous bodily harm–and assault against his wife.

The couple divorced in 2012.

Assault wasn't only red flag

Although Kelley was discharged from the military in such a way that he should have been blackballed from gun purchases, there were other offenses that were equally egregious.

While awaiting his 2012 court-martial, Kelley was housed at Peak Behavioral Health Systems in Santa Teresa, New Mexico.

According to those who later treated him, Kelley never forgot about his desire for vengeance against the military officers who lowered his rank.

Xavier Alvarez, a former Peak Behavioral employee, said that while Kelley was at the facility, he talked a lot about wanting to get revenge over his commanding officers for his discharge.

Other patients reported suspicious activity on the facility's computers, which were restricted to paying bills, and found that Kelley was ordering weapons, magazines, and tactical gear, having it shipped to a P.O. Box in San Antonio.

Alvarez said Kelley was one of the only patients with whom he was unable to form a connection.

"This kid, he was hollow," Alvarez said. "I could never reach him."

One night, sometime after officials had realized that he had been stockpiling weaponry away from the facility, Kelley escaped by jumping a fence in the middle of the night.

Staff immediately began questioning other patients about Kelley.

"It turned out that several times he had mentioned he was practicing for a 12-mile run," Alvarez said. "So, I asked Siri, 'What is the distance to the Greyhound station?'"

Siri's answer? Twelve miles.

Alvarez and police backup headed to the bus station, where they saw Kelley getting out of a cab.

They immediately restrained him.

Although he didn't put up a fight during his arrest, he did say that if he had been given an opportunity, he would have attempted to acquire one of the arresting officer's guns.

End of confinement doesn't lead to reform

Kelley was taken back to the facility but was eventually discharged for his court-martial.

In addition to a bad conduct discharge, his rank was reduced to E-1, airman basic.

After he was released from confinement, he moved into an apartment he'd set up in a barn on his family's property in his rural hometown of New Braunfels, Texas.

His first hint of trouble there was an alleged sexual assault that occurred at his home in June of 2013, with his first wife listed as a witness to the event.

According to Sheriff Mark Reynolds, who was not sheriff at the time, deputies investigated the case for about three months after being called to Kelley's home but stopped investigating after they learned Kelley had left Texas and moved to Colorado. The case has been untouched since October of 2013, Reynolds said, when "it just kind of stalled out."

Kelley had temporarily relocated to Colorado, where he was charged with misdemeanor animal cruelty after a neighbor reported seeing him punch a dog.

Kelley denied the charges but paid more than $500 in fines and restitution.

He retreated back to his hometown of New Braunfels. There, he started dating Danielle Shields, who would in April 2014–when she was 19 and he was 23–become his second wife.

Before they made it to the altar, however, a friend of Shields' called the Comal County Sheriff's Office to report a domestic violence situation between Shields and Kelley.

Once police arrived, however, they were told that the incident was nothing more than a "misunderstanding and teenage drama."

That case, another domestic incident, also didn't prevent Kelley from securing weapons.

"Why didn't someone put two and two together?" Sheriff Mark Reynolds said. "That's what my office is trying to investigate."

The two were married two months later.

Kelley had recently started a job as an unarmed security guard at Summit Vacation Resort, and although he had only been there for five weeks, co-workers said he was quiet but polite.

Manager Claudia Varjabedian said that everyone at the resort was shocked when Kelley didn't turn up for work, until they turned on the news and learned why.

Kelley had previously worked security at Schlitterbahn Waterpark and Resort, also in New Braunfels, but he had been fired from that position.

Signs of trouble came early

While friends from high school don't remember Devin Kelley as angry during his early years, eventually, that changed, and the once happy kid turned darker and more dangerous.

"His parents had him on high doses of 'psych' meds from 6th to 9th grade, the time I knew him," said one of his former classmates.

He was also under a lot of pressure to perform, and that may have made him behave erratically.

He responded by lashing out at others, verbally threatening his classmates when he became angry, one classmate said.

"He used to be happy at one point, normal, your average kid," said a former classmate, Courtney Kleiber, on Facebook. "Over the years we all saw him change into something that he wasn't. To be completely honest, I'm really not surprised this happened, and I don't think anyone who knew him is very surprised, either. My heart goes out to all of the victims that should've never been."

In high school, Kelley became verbally threatening when he got angry, though no one ever thought he'd actually act on those threats, another classmate recalled.

Later, Kelley's Facebook posts were centered around two things—guns and gun violence and atheism—both of which caused his social media relationships to be a bit volatile.

His former high school classmate, Christopher Leo Longoria, unfriended Kelley on Facebook due to his erratic behavior on the social media platform.

That behavior, however, was common since childhood, when he faced pressure from his father to perform well on the football field, his friends said.

According to one friend, Kelley's father would go "crazy" if his son messed up on the field.

What caused Kelley to snap?

While many—including President Donald Trump—have called the mass shooting a mental health issue, experts say that domestic violence is a more telling indicator of the potential for gun violence.

"A history of violent behavior is a far better predictor of future violence than mental illness," said Jeffrey Swanson, a professor in psychiatry and behavioral sciences at Duke University who specializes in gun violence and mental illness.

"We could have better criteria for buying guns based on actual risk and legal tools to remove guns based on risk," Swanson said.

According to a 2014 study by Everytown for Gun Safety, more than half of the mass shootings in the United States between January of 2009 and June of 2014 involved the killing of a partner or family member, and nine of the nation's top ten deadliest shootings in the past fifty years were committed by men with histories of domestic violence.

"Men who feel free to hurt the people they know develop a sense of entitlement to hurt those they don't," wrote Soraya Chemaly in the Village Voice.

Church's pastor returns with words of hope

First Baptist's pastor, Frank Pomeroy, offered comfort to survivors following the attack, which killed his 14-year-old daughter, Annabelle.

"Christ is the one who is going to be lifted up, and that's what I am telling everybody. You lean into what you don't understand. You lean into the Lord," Pomeroy added. "Whatever life brings to you, lean onto the Lord rather than your own understanding. I don't understand, but I know my God does."

The victims:

- Annabelle Pomeroy, 14. Pomeroy, a seventh-grader at Briesemeister Middle School, was the daughter of First Baptist Church's pastor, Frank Pomeroy. The pastor and his wife, Sherri, were out of town the day of the shooting, but their youngest daughter attended services. "One thing that gives me a sliver of encouragement is that Belle was surrounded yesterday by her church family that she loved fiercely and vice versa," Sherri Pomeroy said. "As senseless as this tragedy was, our Belle would not have been able to deal with losing so much family yesterday."

- Bryan and Karla Holcombe. Bryan Holcombe, the church's associate pastor, was walking toward the sanctuary podium to lead services when the shooting began. Bryan also did prison ministry, and it was a path that he had followed since he was a child. "We knew when he was born, that he was going to be a preacher," his father, Joe Holcombe, said in an interview with the Washington Post. "His first word was God." Bryan's wife, Karla, was also dedicated to service. The Holcombes had owned a canvas repair shop in Floresville, Texas, that they had donated to another church for use as a youth center.

- Crystal Holcombe, 36, and her children, Emily Hill, 11, Megan Hill, 8, and Greg Hill, 13. Crystal Holcombe, the mother of five children, was eight months pregnant when she died while seated in a church pew. A widow, Crystal had married John Holcombe–Bryan Holcombe's brother–in 2012, a year after her first husband passed away, leaving her the single mother of five. Three of the children from her first marriage also died in the shooting. "They had actually just found out [about the pregnancy]," said Crystal's aunt, Michele Hill. "They didn't think it was possible so this was just a miracle baby." Emily, Megan and Greg Hill, three of Crystal Holcombe's children, were also killed in the attack. John and Crystal's 7-year-old daughter, Evelyn, was injured in the shooting but has been discharged from the hospital. Crystal's 15-year-old son, Philip, had not been in church that day. According to John Holcombe, they did not know the sex of the baby, but had picked out a name–Carlin Brite "Billy Bob" Holcombe. "This includes Crystal's pick for a girl, a boy, and the nickname the kids gave the baby. Crystal was very thoughtful when coming up with these names. Carlin means

242

small champion. 'Billy Bob' is the nickname the kids gave the baby," John said in a post on Facebook.

- Marc Daniel Holcombe, 36, and his infant daughter, Noah, 18 months. Marc Daniel Holcombe, the son of Bryan and Karla Holcombe, was known as "Danny" by his friends. He died along with his 18-month-old daughter, Noah, attempting to shield his wife and child from the gunman's bullets.

- Joann Ward and her children, Emily Garza, 7, and Brooke Ward, 5. On what was her sixth wedding anniversary, Joann Ward was expecting to have a picnic in the park with her family to celebrate the union. Instead, she died attempting to shield her children from the gunman with her body, saving two of her children, Ryland, Chris's son from a first marriage, and Rihanna. "I didn't get shot because I was hiding, and mama covered Emily, Ryland, and Brooke," Rihanna said after the shooting, according to a family friend. Rihanna said Kelley shot her mother numerous times, as if he was not only making sure that she was dead, but also that the children hidden beneath her also died. Ward's husband, Chris, a truck driver, was at home asleep after working the night shift, when his brother, Michael, woke him up to tell him about the incident, and didn't believe the news at first. "He was pissed at me," Michael told the Dallas Morning News. "I said, 'I'm not lying to you, Chris, they're all shot."

- Lula Woicinski White, 71. White was the grandmother of the gunman's wife, so she likely saw the man responsible for her death and recognized him instantly. White was a widow; her husband had passed away in July. "My sister was a wonderful, caring person—a God-loving person. She loved the people in her church. They were all her best friends," said Mary Mishler Clyburn. "The whole family's devastated, but my sister knew God, and I know that's where she went. That's giving me strength."

- Scott and Karen Marshall, 56 and 57. These Air Force retirees were visiting First Baptist Church of Sutherland to see if it was a good fit for them when they were shot during services. The two had been working separately–Scott Marshall at Lackland Air Force Base in San Antonio, and Karen Marshall at Andrews Air Force Base in Maryland–but now were retiring to Texas. The couple, together for more than 30 years, is survived by a son, two daughters and five grandchildren.

- Tara Elyse McNulty, 33. McNulty, the mother of two children, had moved to Texas from Louisiana two years ago, leaving behind her best friend, Amber Maricle, who asked her regularly to move back to the Pelican State almost every time they talked. "She was all about her kids. Her kids were her No. 1. She was lively, sarcastic, everybody's best friend. My soul sister. We just got each other," Maricle said. Both of McNulty's children were injured but are expected to survive, Maricle added.

- Haley Krueger, 16. Krueger loved children and had future plans to become a nurse on a neonatal intensive care unit, according to her mother, Charlotte Uhl.

- Robert and Shani Corrigan. These Michigan natives were high school sweethearts and the parents of three sons, Forrest, Preston and Benjamin. Forrest, 25, died of suicide in November of 2016, with his funeral service held at First Baptist Church. They were very involved in their church, and Robert was retired from the Air Force.

- Richard and Theresa Rodriguez. Richard was retired from the railroad, and both he and his wife were very involved in their church. "If they were not at church, they'd be in the backyard working on a garden. They were amazing people," said Richard's daughter, Regina Amador, about her father and stepmother.

- Dennis and Sara Johnson. The Johnsons, Dennis, 77, and Sara, 68, had been married for 44 years when they died during church services. The two are survived by their six children as well as several beloved grandchildren, and were expecting four great-grandchildren.

- Keith Braden, 62. Braden was attending church with his wife, Debbie, and their six-year-old granddaughter, Zoe, when he was shot and killed. Both Debbie and Zoe were injured, and Zoe may lose the use of her leg. According to Keith's brother, Bruce Braden, Keith had recently recovered after years of cancer treatment. "He was hoping to have a nice number of years left to live with his family," Bruce Braden said. "That was taken away in an instant."

- Peggy Lynn Warden, 56. Warden, a volunteer Bible School teacher, died attempting to shield her grandson, 18-year-old Zachary Poston, who was shot six times but survived. "My sister, as someone who would serve and protect, put her body over his when the shooting started," her brother, Jimmy Stevens, said. "And that's when she got shot."

Witnesses were also at risk

Kevin Jordan was changing the oil in his car when he heard Kelley shooting.

"I look up and I see this guy, and he's shooting as he's walking towards the church," Jordan said. "He was wearing either body armor or a vest and a mask, and I couldn't see his face or anything, and I saw him shooting and he just kept going, kept going.

"When I was trying to run back inside my house ... he saw me, and he took a shot off in my direction, and it went through the front window of my house. And my two-year-old son ... he was standing in the window, two feet from where it hit," Jordan said. "It almost hit him. I grabbed my son, and grabbed my wife, and we barricaded ourselves in the bathroom and I called 911."

He did not look out until he heard shots that did not sound like the gunman's. That's when he saw his friend and neighbor, barefoot and confronting the suspect.

"It's one of the worst things that I've ever seen, and it's going to haunt me for a very, very long time," Jordan said. "It's people that I know, that are friends. Why would you choose a church of people that are just with their families praying on Sunday?"

After the shooting

Kelley may have thought that he would leave the church unnoticed, but many neighbors in addition to Jordan heard the rapid-fire hail of bullets, and one man–Stephen Willeford, a plumber who lives near the church–ran barefoot to the scene, carrying his AR-15.

Willeford, a former National Rifle Association instructor, had been napping when his daughter woke him up to tell him she heard shooting. Instinctively, Willeford grabbed his rifle and ran out the door.

"I kept hearing the shots, one after another, very rapid shots—just 'pop, pop, pop, pop'—and I knew every one of those shots represented someone, that it was aimed at someone, that they weren't just random shots," Willeford said.

When he got to the church, he almost immediately encountered Kelley and took cover behind a pickup truck and exchanged gunfire with the shooter.

According to authorities, at least one of Willeford's shots connected.

"We know that the suspect was shot," said Freeman Martin of the Texas Department of Public Safety. "When he dropped his assault rifle, jumped in his Ford Expedition, and fled the scene, this good Samaritan, our Texas hero, flagged down another young man and jumped in his vehicle and they pursued the suspect."

That man was Johnnie Langendorff, on his way to visit his girlfriend when he saw a man in a mask exchanging gunfire with the barefooted Willeford before the masked man jumped into his vehicle and drove away.

"The gentleman with the rifle came across the street, opened my door, and said, 'He shot up the church and we've got to chase him,'" Langendorff told CNN in an interview. "I said, 'Let's go.' That's what you do. You, you chase a bad guy."

Speeds reach nearly 100 miles per hour during the 15-minute chase, which ended when Kelly crashed his SUV into a ditch.

"I didn't know if anyone had a clue or not which direction he had gone," added Langendorff, who said they called authorities and alerted them to Kelley's location during the chase. "I know that all the police were coming to the church to help, but, you know, I wanted to pursue him to make sure he got caught."

After he crashed his vehicle, Kelley failed to exit after the two erstwhile heroes called out to him, and he was confirmed dead at the scene when police arrived. He is believed to have died of a self-inflicted gunshot wound, although Willeford did shoot him twice before he escaped from the scene of the church shooting.

Before taking his own life, police said Kelley called his father to tell him that he'd been shot and likely would not survive.

"We are grieving, our family is grieving," Michael Kelley later said from his New Braunfels home, 35 miles north of Sutherland Springs. "I don't want our lives, our grandchildren's lives, destroyed by this media circus."

Willeford and Langendorff had never before met, but they both had the same mission in mind.

"There was no thinking about it. There was just doing. That was the key to all this. Act now. Ask questions later," Langendorff said.

At the church, the scene was a nightmare, first responders say

Mike Shaw and his wife, Jamie, both EMTs with La Vernia Emergency Medical Service, were the first to arrive after the shooting at First Baptist Church, and the blood-soaked sanctuary continues to haunt them.

"I'm trying to get the horror out of my mind," paramedic Mike Shaw told NBC News. "But you can't unsee what you already saw."

Inside were twenty-six victims, a third of them children, and twenty more wounded. The congregation had been decimated, and both parents and children were screaming, some in desperation over the loss of their loved ones, others in pain from multiple gunshot wounds.

"For something like that, there's no real training for it," he added. "Absolute horror. As far as the people, I think I knew a few of them."

Still, the couple fought through their shock and remained as professional as possible, despite the body count that turned the church into a battlefield.

"It's chaos, but you just have to fly through that mentality and just zone-in on all your aspects," said EMS Chief Paul Brunner, who immediately sped to the church as soon as he heard what had happened, praying the entire way. "You can't just get wrapped-up in the chaos."

Still, the number of children killed in the incident was particularly shocking.

"Our inclination is to protect children. The thing is, that wasn't his inclination," Brunner said. "He wasn't separating going: 'I'm not going to hurt the kids. I'm going to go after whatever adults wronged me.'"

248

Instead, many of his targets were children, which was devastating for anyone at the church that day.

After treating the survivors, the Shaws went home and hugged their three children.

They still struggle with flashbacks, however.

"You have dreams, nightmares," said Mike Shaw.

Rebecca Metcalf was normally on call with the Shaws but was off that day. Later, she discovered that her father, Keith Braden, had been killed, and her mother, Debbie, and six-year-old niece, Zoe, had been wounded in the attack.

"I'm trying to get the horror out of my mind," Metcalf said. "I've been so busy trying to get everything taken care of and trying to help out with family and all that I still don't think I've had time to register everything. My sister works with a lot of the kids at the church, so not only is she dealing with Zoe being in the hospital, she's dealing with all the babies that she helped take care of that are gone."

Messages of support and prayer have come from all over the world, Metcalf added.

"So now everybody knows, everybody knows where Sutherland Springs is, and it sucks that this is the reason why," she said.

Kelley was practicing before shooting

Like the run he'd trained for before escaping from the military mental facility, Kelley practiced before his church shooting.

Neighbor Ryan Albers, 16, said he heard regular gunfire coming from his neighbor's property.

"At first, I thought someone was blasting," Albers said. "It had to be coming from somewhere pretty close. It was definitely not just a shotgun or someone hunting. It was someone using automatic weapon fire."

Another neighbor, Robert Gonzalez, said that in the week before the church shooting, he heard gunfire coming from Kelley's property every morning.

He noticed the gunshots, which he identified as a .45 or an assault rifle, based on his own military experience, because they were so close to the house. And while target practice isn't unusual in the rural region of Texas, he took notice because of the unusual amount of gunfire.

The previous record

Previously, the deadliest mass shooting in Texas history happened in 1991 at Luby's Cafeteria in Killeen, Texas, when George Hennard drove his pickup truck through the restaurant's window on Boss's Day, then rapidly began shooting restaurant patrons, killing 23 people and wounding 27 more.

"All women of Killeen and Belton are vipers! This is what you've done to me and my family! This is what Bell County did to me. This is payback day!" yelled Hennard before he opened fire, using both a 9mm Glock 17 pistol and a 9mm Ruger P89 pistol as his weapons.

Hennard, who had mainly targeted women during the carnage at the restaurant, later shot himself in the head after barricading himself in the restaurant bathroom.

HEAD OF MANSON FAMILY DIES AT 83

Charles Manson thought he would become a rock star, if only because of his relationship with Dennis Wilson, who in the summer of 1968, found himself as much mesmerized by Manson as other members of what was dubbed "the family."

"This is Charlie," Wilson told friends. "He is the wizard, man. He is a gas."

They spent that summer dropping acid, jamming, and having group sex, until things took a dangerous turn, and the two split apart.

A year later, Manson's family had moved on from innocent dumpster diving to feed their communal lifestyle of sex, drugs, and rock and roll to a murder spree that left nine dead, including actress Sharon Tate.

Dennis Wilson had one tie to Manson–a song that the cult leader had written that the Beach Boys had altered somewhat and recorded–but refused to discuss their time together.

"As long as I live," Wilson later told Rolling Stone, "I'll never talk about that."

On November 19, Manson died at a Bakersfield hospital, a week after turning 83, bringing a degree of closure to those who lost loved ones during what was eventually dubbed the Manson Family Murders.

Manson already had a lengthy record sparked by rough childhood

Manson was born in 1934 to a single mother and had already spent half his life behind bars when he began forming his "family," a response to the coming race wars he dubbed "Helter Skelter" after a

Beatles song that he believed were on the horizon and would lead to the end of the world, unless something equally horrible happened to stop it.

He wanted to be the one to be hailed a hero, so he and his family put his plan into action, only to end up on death row, all victims of Manson's psychotic, paranoid thoughts.

Manson was born to 16-year-old Kathleen Manson-Bower-Cavender (née Maddox), just a few months after she'd married her first husband, William Eugene Manson, a laborer at a dry-cleaning business. (Manson's own father, Colonel Walker Henderson Scott Sr., the Colonel just for show, was a con artist who walked out on his mother as soon as she told him she was pregnant.)

Maddox wasn't a fan of marriage and motherhood, however, and she spent much of her time drinking with her brother, Luther, leaving young Charles (initially named no-name Maddox until William Manson agreed to allow the boy to take his name) to be tended to by babysitters.

Within a few years, however, the elder Manson realized Kathleen was not much of a mother or wife, and the two divorced in 1937.

Two years later, Maddox was arrested after she and her brother's girlfriend, Julia Vickers, were drinking with a man named Frank Martin, who they decided to rob along with Luther's help. Charles was sent to live with an aunt and uncle in West Virginia until his mother was paroled in 1942.

Despite her absenteeism as a mother, Manson said the time spent with his mother after she was paroled was among the happiest he'd ever experienced.

That should come as no surprise, because Manson's childhood was a free-for-all.

Manson and his mother moved to Charleston, where Manson rarely went to school, instead spending his time stealing from stores and his home.

He eventually established a routine of moving from schools for boys to juvenile facilities to reform schools, where at one Manson said he was raped by several of the other boys housed at the facility.

After spending time in more strict institutions, he was finally released at the age of 21. A year later, he married a waitress, Rosalie Jean Willis, who soon became pregnant with their son, Charles Manson Jr.

A car theft and subsequent parole violations led to three years behind bars at Terminal Island in San Pedro, California, where Rosalie and his mother, living in Los Angeles to help raise Charles Jr. together, visited together for the first year, until Rosalie started seeing another man. Manson was so enraged by the news he attempted to break out by stealing a car, just two weeks before a parole hearing.

He did not get another chance at parole until 1958, when Rosalie asked for and received a divorce.

Shortly thereafter, he married a prostitute named Leona (her working name was Candy Stevens) most likely so she would not be requested to testify against Manson in court, as charges began piling up, including pimping out underage girls and attempting to cash a forged U.S. Treasury check.

Guitar lessons set future path

While being held at the United States Federal Penitentiary at McNeil Island, he began taking guitar lessons from Alvin "Creepy" Karpis, head of the Barker-Karpis gang, the only FBI "Public Enemy Number One" to be taken alive. (The others, John Dillinger, Pretty Boy Floyd, and Baby Face Nelson, were all dead at the time of their capture). The Barker-Karpis gang included the infamous "Ma"

Barker, although she, according to Karpis, participated in none of their nefarious activities.

"Ma was always somebody in our lives. Love didn't enter into it really. She was somebody we looked after and took with us when we moved city to city, hideout to hideout. It is no insult to Ma's memory that she just didn't have the know-how to direct us on a robbery. It would not have occurred to her to get involved in our business, and we always made it a point of only discussing our scores when Ma wasn't around. We'd leave her at home when we were arranging a job, or we'd send her to a movie. Ma saw a lot of movies," he said.

Karpis spent the most time of any other prisoner at Alcatraz, 26 years, and also spent time at Leavenworth before landing at McNeil Island, where he met Charles Manson, who wanted to learn to play guitar so he could become a rock star.

Karpis, however, didn't think "Little Charlie" had it in him.

He "is so lazy and shiftless, I doubt if he'll put in the time required to learn," Karpis said.

Still, given his background–time in orphanages, reformatories and federal prison and a prostitute for a mother–made Karpis reconsider.

"I decide it's time someone did something for him, and to my surprise, he learns quickly. He has a pleasant voice and a pleasing personality, although he's unusually meek and mild for a convict. He never has a harsh word to say and is never involved in even an argument," Karpis later wrote about the experience of teaching Manson to play guitar in the book, "On the Rock: Twenty-Five Years in Alcatraz," which he wrote with Robert Livesey.

Manson told Karpis that he was going to be bigger than the Beatles, and in some ways, he certainly did become more infamous than the famed British rock group that fell apart before fans had finished catapulting them to fame.

During the time of guitar lessons and big dreams, his second wife Leona, despite having given birth to Manson's second son, Charles Luther, asked him for a divorce. It was in 1963, several years before he was finally released from federal prison, despite his odd request to stay.

When he finally was released in 1967, he immediately headed to California, where the guitar lessons he'd taken from one of the nation's most notorious gangsters would surely pay off.

When Manson met Wilson

Manson had already started forming his family when he met Dennis Wilson.

He gathered his groupies in San Francisco's Haight-Asbury district, where many aimless young people found themselves during the era of peace and love.

Manson was charismatic and was able to lure people into his fold rather easily and then held them there with sex, drugs, and promises.

It was actually one of the family members who made it happen.

"Charlie told us that all we had to do was ask the universe for what we wanted and it would be presented," wrote Dianne Lake, in her memoir, "Member of the Family," released a few weeks before Manson's death. (Lake did not participate in the LaBianca-Tate murders, which would give Manson the infamy he sought.)

"In the connection with Dennis Wilson, it appeared that was precisely what had happened," she added. "Charlie had led us to the communal promised land—everything he'd asked for had come to pass. Charlie's beliefs … were being validated more and more each day. Just the fact that he'd been able to captivate someone as famous as a member of the Beach Boys was proof enough."

On the day Manson met the Beach Boy, Wilson was driving down Sunset Boulevard when he saw two girls who were hitchhiking,

Patricia Krenwinkel and Ella Jo Bailey, and decided to give them a ride.

They told him they were headed to the home of their spiritual guru, a musician named Charlie, and Wilson, struggling with a divorce as well as the unwelcome elements of fame, was intrigued.

"Dennis and Charlie hit it off right away, which is not surprising, given Charlie's skills at ingratiating himself with strangers," Lake wrote in her memoir. "Dennis, in no rush to leave, hung out for a while, smoked some pot with Charlie, and listened a bit to Charlie's songs. It was obvious from the start that Dennis liked the girls and admired Charlie's harem. We sat at Charlie's feet and looked at him lovingly as he sang and played guitar. We made sure Dennis saw how much we idolized Charlie—we knew that was our job, without Charlie even having to tell us."

Manson even showed Wilson, a self-taught drummer, some chords on the guitar while they passed around joints and chatted.

Dennis and Charlie hit it off so well that it was only a few days later before Manson and his girls had moved into Wilson's Malibu bachelor pad, where they did drugs and engaged in group sex, until a nasty bout of gonorrhea struck everyone, requiring Wilson to take his new friends to a doctor for treatment.

Despite living an upscale life with Wilson, Manson and his family wanted to show him some of their survival skills.

"That is how we wound up driving in Dennis's burgundy Rolls-Royce to the back of a grocery store and showed him the art of dumpster diving," wrote Lake. "We all laughed and sang all the way to the dumpster, dragging Dennis by his hand. The best thing we found on this run was a flat of strawberries. After culling out the bad ones, we had enough to make him a strawberry cake complete with fresh Cool Whip. Charlie was leaning against the Rolls watching as we showed Dennis how it was done. 'Dennis, do you know how

256

much good food is thrown out in America?' he shouted. One of the girls popped a fresh strawberry into Dennis's mouth and we all hopped back in the car. That night the girls and I made an entire meal with the produce and other discarded food. Then we presented Dennis with his cake."

Late in the summer, Wilson invited Manson to come to the studio to record some music, and what should have been an opportunity of a lifetime turned sour quickly when Manson failed to appreciate suggestions from Wilson and the producers including Terry Melcher, and eventually pulled out a knife.

Later, Wilson exacerbated the situation by recording with the Beach Boys, a version of one of Manson's songs, "Cease to Exist," which Manson had written specifically for the group and had received compensation. Wilson, however, changed some of the lyrics and renamed it "Never Learn Not to Love." Wilson was credited as the only writer.

Manson and his followers moved out, but not long after, according to Beach Boys collaborator Van Dyke Parks, the two reunited, at least for a while.

"One day, Charles Manson brought a bullet out and showed it to Dennis, who asked, 'What's this?' And Manson replied, 'It's a bullet. Every time you look at it, I want you to think how nice it is your kids are still safe.'" Later, Manson said, "I gave him a bullet because he changed the words to my song."

Manson family settled in at 'the ranch'

The incident with Dennis Wilson changed the elements of peace and love that existed for the Manson family, which settled on an abandoned film set, Spahn Ranch, which was a mountainous region perfect for filming westerns including "Bonanza," "The Lone Ranger," and "Zorro," among others.

The family was allowed to stay rent-free in exchange for helping 80-year-old George Spahn maintain the 500-acre property.

Here, he made the girls on the ranch feel special, which led virtually all of them to fall in love with him.

"He made you feel like you were his one and only love, you know?" Lake said in an interview with "Good Morning America. "And yes, there were other girls, but we all shared him. He made you feel really special, and specially loved."

Although Lake was just 14 when they met at a party in Topanga, California, and Manson was 34, they had sex within hours of that initial meeting.

"I needed love and affection, and I needed a family. I needed to feel like I belonged somewhere," Lake said. "And he perceived that from the get-go. It seemed very natural and loving and kind of like a game. He was cute, impish. You know, fun."

And initially, aside from the bullet he handed Wilson as a threat, the Manson family mischief only involved going into people's homes to rearrange their furniture, just to let them know that someone had invaded their personal space.

Ramblings turn to violence

Eventually, however, Manson's ramblings about "Helter Skelter" turned violent, and he worked harder to lure in the family, which he had manipulated with LSD, playing the Beatles' "White Album" (songs included "Dear Prudence," "Blackbird," "Back in the U.S.S.R.," "Don't Pass Me By," "Why Don't We Do It in The Road" and "Happiness is a Warm Gun," among others) constant Bible verse readings, and lectures, according to Leslie Van Houton.

"A typical day would be Charlie playing guitar, telling stories, dancing around just being free," said Linda Kasabian, who was 20 with a 16-month-old child when she found Manson.

First victim died for money

Gary Hinman befriended members of the Manson family and often invited them to hang out at his house in Topanga Canyon, where they played music and did drugs. For some reason, Manson believed that Hinman, who had discovered Buddhism and was planning a religious pilgrimage to Asia, had bonds and other valuables in his house, and on July 25, 1968, he sent Manson family members Bobby Beausoleil, Susan Atkins, and Mary Brunner to Hinman's place to convince Gary to not only join the family, but also to sign over all of his assets.

"Bruce [Davis] drove and just dropped us off," said Mary Brunner. "We decided that Sadie (Susan Atkins) and I would go to the house and if Gary was there alone, we'd signal at the window. We were going to ask Gary for some money—for $3,000 or $30,000—I'm not sure how much. Bobby asked Gary for the money, and Gary said he didn't have any. Bobby said we weren't kidding and pulled out the gun and there was a fight."

That fight turned into a three-day ordeal during which Manson and Davis, who Manson met while dabbling briefly in Scientology, stopped by, Manson carrying a sword he used to slash Hinman's face and ear.

Hinman asked them all to leave, but only Manson and Davis departed. The others stayed, Atkins and Brunner stitching Hinman's ear with dental floss, and tortured him until the 27th, when, only after Hinman signed over two of his cars, Beausoleil stabbed him twice in the chest, and then all three took turns pressing a pillow into his face until he stopped breathing.

Hinman prayed the entire time.

After he was dead, the trio wrote "Political Piggy" on the wall in Hinman's blood and drew a paw print in an attempt to make it appear as though the Black Panthers were responsible for the murder.

Bobby Beausoleil was quickly arrested for Gary Hinman's murder after falling asleep in one of Hinman's stolen cars.

Manson decided that some copycat murders were in order to help spring Beausoleil from prison.

What followed was just as awful.

First blood fuels frenzy

On August 9, 1969, Manson sent his followers to 10050 Cielo Drive in Benedict Canyon, a home that was being rented by actress Sharon Tate ("The Valley of the Dolls") and her husband, director Roman Polanski, for an evening of murder and mayhem. Tate was eight-and-a-half months pregnant.

While Manson himself didn't ride along, he had sent them with distinct instructions–"Destroy everyone in it–as gruesome as you can."–believing that the home was still occupied by Terry Melcher (the son of Doris Day), who had failed to sign Manson for a recording contract, despite his relationship with Dennis Wilson.

"This residence–10050 Cielo Drive–where Tate and Polanski now lived, came to symbolize the establishment to Charles Manson, particularly the establishment's rejection of him," said Vincent Bugliosi, who prosecuted Manson. "Manson–who was uneducated but highly intelligent–had this phenomenal ability to gain control over other people and get them to do terrible things. Eventually he convinced them that he was the second coming: Christ and the Devil all wrapped up in the same person."

And the Devil can make people do dreadful, dreadful things.

"I felt excited, special, chosen," Kasabian said of being selected for the night's murder plot.

Eager for her husband's upcoming return home, Tate had gone out to dinner at her favorite restaurant, El Coyote, with her friends, hairdresser Jay Sebring, coffee heiress Abigail Folger, and Folger's boyfriend, Wojtek Frykowski. They returned home at about 10:30 p.m.

When Manson's four chosen family members–Kasabian, Charles "Tex" Watson, Susan Atkins and Patricia "Katie" Krenwinkel– arrived at 10050 Cielo Drive in Benedict Canyon, the action started immediately.

"When we arrived at the Tate residence, there were lights on the outside, the driveway was lit up. Tex got a rope and wire cutters and cut the telephone wires. There was a car coming so we got down. Tex jumped out and shot the gun four times. He told me to take the wallet from the kid he had shot. I got in the car. There was this person slumped over. I didn't see any blood or anything, but I knew he wasn't there," Kasabian said.

The young man in the car was Steve Parent, a friend of the housekeeper, who was leaving the property.

The three others continued into the house.

Watson accessed the house by cutting a screen and then helped the girls into the house. Once there, all of them on acid, they herded the home's occupants into the living room, lining them up in front of the fireplace. A bit of a fight broke out, and Sebring was shot. This created mass panic in the room, and Frykowski ran out the front door, only to be shot twice and stabbed fifty-one times before being hit over the head more than twelve times with the butt of the pistol.

Folger attempted to flee out a back bedroom door, but she was caught on the lawn and stabbed twenty-eight times, her white dress soon turning crimson from the loss of blood.

"I saw a woman in a white dress and she had blood all over her and she was screaming, and she was calling for her mom. I saw Katie stabbing her," said Linda Kasabian, the lookout for the family that night. "I thought about going to a house where there were lights down the road and then I said, 'No, don't do that, because they'll find me and kill all those people.' So, I went down the hill and I got into the car and I just stayed there and waited."

Police later thought that Folger was wearing a red nightgown, there was so much blood at the scene.

Inside, Tate and Sebring were tied together around their necks with a white cord stretched over a ceiling beam.

Sebring had been shot in the face and stabbed seven times.

Tate was stabbed sixteen times, an X carved into her stomach, and even as she begged for her life and the life of her baby, Atkins yelled back, "I don't care about you or your baby. Woman, I have no mercy for you."

The word "pig" was written on the front door in Sharon Tate's blood.

The only survivor of the carnage was caretaker William Garretson, whose quarters were separate from the main house. He apparently was playing music so loud that he did not hear the screams.

Polanski came home to overwhelming publicity and a sadness that never really left him.

"Even after so many years, I find myself unable to watch a spectacular sunset or visit a lovely old house or experience visual pleasure of any kind without instinctively telling myself how much she would have loved it all," Polanski wrote in the 2004 book "Sharon Tate Recollection," compiled by Tate's sister, Debra Tate.

Another night, another murder

On August 10, 1969, the night after the Tate murder, Manson and six of the Manson family members (Leslie Van Houten, Steve Grogan, Atkins, Kasabian, Krenwinkel, and Watson) again went out into the night to commit another murder, this time to increase the panic he felt was not intense enough after the Tate murders.

The family drove around until they came upon a neighborhood they recognized because Manson and other family members had attended a party there a year earlier.

The house they chose was owned by grocery company owner Leno LaBianca and his wife, Rosemary.

Initially, Manson and Watson went into the house, tying the LaBiancas with lamp cord and covering their heads with pillowcases. Manson told them that they were only being robbed, but as soon as the women entered the house, Manson left and told Van Houten and Krenwinkel to follow Watson's orders. Kasabian was again a lookout.

Watson, Van Houten and Krenwinkel stabbed Rosemary LaBianca 41 times. Leno was stabbed 25 times, and Krenwinkel, perhaps the most depraved of them all, carved the word "war" into his stomach.

In the living room, they wrote "Death to pigs" and "Rise" in Leno LaBianca's blood. On the refrigerator door, they misspelled "Healter Skelter," also in Leno's blood.

The two were discovered by Frank Struthers, Rosemary's son from a previous marriage, and his sister's boyfriend, Joe Dorgan, the next day. They immediately called the LAPD.

A few weeks later, Family murders again

Donald "Shorty" Shea had been working as a handyman at the Spahn Ranch and had been coexisting rather peacefully with Manson and his family until he had agreed to help evict the family because of a raid on the ranch on August 16 that had resulted in the arrests of several family members on suspicion of car theft.

The negative publicity wasn't something Spahn wanted for his former movie set, but the plan for eviction would turn deadly for Shea. Manson believed that Shea had tipped off the police and decided that the 36-year-old stuntman had to die for being a snitch.

In order to kill Shea, Bruce Davis, Tex Watson, and Steve Grogan asked the ranch hand if he could give them a ride to a car parts yard. Davis and Grogan sat in the back, while Watson sat in front next to Shea.

In his confession, Davis said that Grogan made the first move, and hit Shea over the head with a pipe wrench, disorienting him enough that Watson was then able to stab him from the passenger seat.

They then took Shea behind a hill on the ranch and tortured him until he died.

"I was in the backseat with Grogan," Davis said at one of his parole hearings. "They took Shorty out. I stayed in the car for quite a while but … then I went down the hill later on, and that's when I cut Shorty on the shoulder with the knife. I don't know if he was dead or not. He didn't bleed when I cut him on the shoulder."

Other family members, including Charles Manson, were there when Davis arrived at the murder scene.

"When I showed up, Manson handed me a machete as if I was supposed to...I mean I know what he wanted. But you know I couldn't do that. I mean I just couldn't do it. And then I threw the knife. [Manson] handed me a bayonet and it...I just reached over and ... I don't know which side it was on, but I cut him right about here on the shoulder just with the tip of the blade. Sort of like saying 'Are you satisfied, Charlie?' And I turned around and walked away. And I was sick for about two or three days. I mean, I couldn't even think about what I, what I had done."

Despite crime similarities, LAPD was stumped

Police weren't certain of the connection between the Tate and LaBianca murders, despite stark similarities. And it could have been a long time before they tied either event to the Manson family.

But Manson had a plan after Helter Skelter, to survive the coming apocalypse in a secret city hidden beneath Death Valley he dubbed "the bottomless pit." When they emerged from the pit, they would take over the world.

And the family had been spending time between the Spahn Ranch and its movie sets and the Barker Ranch at Death Valley.

And there at the Barker Ranch, as they dug for Manson's bottomless pit, they also burned some equipment that belonged to Death Valley National Monument. That move led to a raid on the ranches of Death Valley, where they found stolen cars and made numerous arrests, including members of the Manson family. Charles Manson was one of those arrested; he was found tucked inside a cabinet beneath a sink.

Family members and others turn out to be a chatty bunch

The first person to talk was Kitty Lutesinger, who was arrested along with the Manson family at the ranches. Lutesinger was Bobby Beausoleil's girlfriend, and upon learning that, they began questioning her about Gary Hinman's murder.

Lutesinger connected Atkins to the Hinman murder; meanwhile, Atkins was spilling all about the Tate murders to her bunkmates in jail.

"When I plunged the knife into her, it made me have an orgasm," Atkins told her cellmate, 31-year-old Shelley Nadell, about the murder of Tate and her unborn baby.

"Those people died not out of hate or anything ugly. I know now it has all been perfect. I am not going to defend our beliefs, I am just telling you the way it is," Atkins added in letters she wrote to Nadell. "In killing someone physically you are only releasing the soul…Death is only an illusion."

Atkins also told another inmate, Virginia Castro, that she killed Sharon Tate, "Because we wanted to do a crime that would shock the world, that the world would have to stand up and take notice."

Soon, detectives found themselves knee-deep in evidence as they took fingerprints and other physical evidence from those in custody and issued arrest warrants for those who were not, including Watson, Kasabian, and Krenwinkel.

Kasabian turned herself in, which opened the door for her to testify against the family in exchange for her own freedom, and Watson and Krenwinkel were arrested based on fingerprint evidence.

"[Kasabian] never asked for immunity from prosecution, but we gave it," prosecutor Vincent Bugliosi said in a 2009 interview with The Guardian. "She stood in the witness box for seventeen or eighteen days and never broke down, despite the incredible pressure she was under. I doubt we would have convicted Manson without her."

During her testimony, she called Manson a "devil, not this wonderful man that I was led to believe."

Many originally were sentenced to death

On December 13, 1971, Charles Manson was convicted of first-degree murder in Los Angeles County Court for the July 25, 1969, murder of Gary Hinman and the August 26, 1969, murder of Donald "Shorty" Shea.

In court, he attempted to remove the blame for the murders from himself, and said, "These children that come at you with knives, they are your children. You taught them; I didn't teach them. I just tried to help them stand up. I have killed no one, and I have ordered no one to be killed."

He was initially sentenced to death, although all death sentences were commuted in 1972, so his sentence was changed to life with the possibility of parole. He was denied parole 12 times. His next hearing would have been in 2027.

He spent time in San Quentin State Prison, California Medical Facility, Folsom State Prison, Pelican Bay State Prison, and California State Prison in Corcoran, his final place of confinement.

On September 25, 1984, while at California Medical Facility at Vacaville, fellow inmate Jan Holmstrom, a Hare Krishna, poured paint thinner on Manson and set him on fire, leaving him with second- and third-degree burns on more than 20 percent of his body. Holmstrom did it because Manson threatened him over his Hare Krishna chants, he said.

More than 30 years later, he died in Mercy Hospital in downtown Bakersfield of natural causes.

After Manson

Patricia Krenwinkel, who is best remembered for laughing while walking into court with two other Manson followers, now understands what led her to the Manson family.

"I wanted to please. I wanted to feel safe. To feel like someone was going to care for me," Krenwinkel said in the documentary "My Life After Manson," a 2014 study of Krenwinkel's life that debuted at the Tribeca Film Festival. "I hadn't felt that from anyone else in my life. In giving up and moving on with Manson, I was just basically throwing away the rest of my life... It is countless how many lives were shattered by the path of destruction that I was a part of, and it all comes from such a simple thing as just wanting to be loved."

While it has been almost 50 years since the Tate-LaBianca murders took place, Manson's death will most certainly revive a fascination for the killings that have never really left.

"Some people point to the extreme brutality of the murders to explain our enduring interest, but you know we have had killings even more brutal in America," said Bugliosi. "And yes, the victims were prominent people, but they weren't that prominent. But what really gives the Tate killings such durability is the fact they are the most bizarre murders in the recorded annals of American crime. If they had been written as fiction no one would have read it. It would have seemed too far out. After all, the story has just about everything–Beatles lyrics spelled out in blood, quotes from the Bible, and nice kids from average families being persuaded to go on horrible killing sprees.

"The very name Manson has now become a metaphor for evil as a result. The name is synonymous with evil today. Mike Tyson, when he was applying for reinstatement of his boxing license, admitted he was a bad guy but insisted 'I am not Charlie Manson.' Certainly, Manson was different from all other mass murderers. He got others to do his work, and he was intelligent and manipulative. Most deranged cult leaders end up getting their followers to commit suicide en masse. Manson got them to carry out mass murders. That is why we remember him."

The aftermath

Manson left all his possessions and the rights to use his name and image, as well as his songs, to a pen pal he began writing to from prison in 2002.

A grandson had hoped to gain custody of Manson's body, but Manson deliberately disowned all his family members, giving the pen pal the right to claim his body within 10 days of Manson's death.

He otherwise would be cremated by the California prison system.

THANKSGIVING WAS A BLOODY FEAST FOR ONE VIRGINIA FAMILY

On his Facebook page, Christopher Gattis is standing with his arm around his wife, Jeanett Lau Gattis, in front of the Biltmore estate in Asheville, North Carolina, a few hours from his home in Chester, Virginia, where he's worked as a youth pastor since 2014 at Grace Lutheran Church.

His profile picture, also of himself and his wife, was also from 2014, although they were dressed for a black-tie event, and friends commented on how great the two of them looked.

"Yea! I just wish we could stay looking like that. Lol," responded Gattis, who was charged with three counts of first-degree murder and three counts of using a firearm in the commission of a felony when a Thanksgiving Day domestic dispute got out of hand.

Victims were surprised by gunshots

Gattis, 58, and his wife got married in 2009, a lavish affair during which the bride wore a white lace gown with a halter top and the groom wore a tuxedo with a bow tie.

Throughout the marriage, both appeared happy.

Jeanett Lau Gattis, 58, regularly posted pics of her grandchildren and also posted selfies with her daughter, 30-year-old Candice Kunze, who went by the nickname Candy.

Both Jeanett and Candy were killed in the Thanksgiving domestic dispute, as was Candy's boyfriend, 36-year-old Andrew Buthorn.

Officials said the women's bodies were found inside the home and the man's body was found in the front yard.

Gattis is being held without bond at the Chesterfield County Jail.

Neighbors were surprised by event

"We were all friends," said neighbor Mike Brown, who lived in the Dogwood Ridge Court block of the Ashley Forrest subdivision of Chester, Virginia, where the families would often have cookouts.

"I had no clue that they were having problems that I knew of, but behind closed doors is behind closed doors," he said.

Another neighbor said that Jeanett's daughter and boyfriend had moved into the home about six weeks ago, which could have led to the problems.

Neighbors described the events in a surreal way, as if they had never expected to hear gunfire on Thanksgiving.

Darius Williams was outside with his nephew the day of the shooting when they heard the bang. Williams' nephew thought it was a firecracker, but Williams knew it was a gunshot.

He didn't think much about it, though, until flashing police lights turned the cul-de-sac into a crime scene, especially as the lights illuminated Buthorn's body, which was left in the yard for hours as police processed the crime scene.

"I looked at that body all night," said Denise Patton, Larry's wife. "I didn't know who it was."

Church responds

Cristopher Gattis had been the high school youth ministries coordinator for Grace Lutheran Church for several years, and his arrest left church members shocked and saddened.

"Grace Lutheran Church has experienced many hardships over the years, but this heartbreak has unique challenges, the church said in a statement. "Grace Lutheran Church asks for the prayers from our community as our congregation begins the process of addressing the grief being experienced by everyone involved."

Other Thanksgiving murders

In 2009, 35-year-old Paul Michael Merhige of Miami killed four of his family members after enjoying a Thanksgiving meal with his family.

Merhige killed his twin sisters, Carla and Lisa Knight, 33, his 79-year-old aunt, Raymonde Joseph, and the six-year-old daughter of his cousin, Makayla Sitton, who was asleep in her bed when she was killed by a stray bullet.

After opening fire, Merhige was heard saying he had waited 20 years to kill them, according to the family member who had hosted the dinner at his Jupiter, Florida, home.

"We know the suspect had an ongoing resentment toward family members and at some point in the evening left the residence for a short period of time, then returned and started shooting without warning," Jupiter Police Sgt. Scott Pascarella said.

"He had this whole thing pre-planned. His goal was to shoot his sisters and punish his parents," said Jim Sitton, whose daughter's death was likely collateral damage, as there was no reason for her to be targeted.

Pascarella said there were seventeen guests at the holiday dinner massacre at the Sitton home, which happened after Merhige had enjoyed the meal with his family.

A neighbor called 911 after family members escaped the house in search of help.

When Sitton had tucked his daughter Makayla into bed that night, they had talked about her upcoming role in the Nutcracker ballet, which was scheduled for the next night.

"She was very excited about this," he said. "She's just, our life, and I don't know how we're ever going to recover."

In 2013, Rachel Hutson shot and killed her 58-year-old mother,

Susan Lee Hutson, In Chesapeake, Virginia, only hours after finishing Thanksgiving dinner, then sent a picture of the woman's dead body to her father via text message.

At the time of the shooting, Hutson was serving as a full-time caregiver for her mother, who was terminally ill.

Her father had gone out to do some Black Friday shopping when the shooting occurred.

Rachel went into her mother's room in the early morning hours after Thanksgiving with a gun, firing shots until her ears were ringing. The woman who had suffered from congestive heart failure, kidney failure, and diabetes, the woman who had given birth to Rachel, was dead.

"I told her that I was sorry," Rachel said on an episode of "The Dr. Phil Show," adding that her mother had told her she was "crazy" as soon as she spotted the gun in her daughter's hand.

"I don't think she realized what had happened," said Rachel, who said that she could tell that her mother was dead, because she wasn't moving. "I told her I was sorry, I just kept saying I was sorry."

She then debated killing herself too, but instead sent a text to her father, Donald, telling him what she had done. Her cell phone immediately rang, her panicked father on the other end of the line.

"I told him that I had shot mom," Rachel said. "He thought I was trying to upset him. He hung up and he called on my mom's phone, and I answered that phone too and told him, again, what I did. He kept telling me to put mom on the phone, and I kept telling him that she was dead. He still didn't believe me."

That was when she sent him the photo of her mother, dead in bed.

"I wanted him to believe me because every second of reality was unbearable," she said.

According to Rachel's sister, Sarah, Rachel was prone to "fits of rage" that could have easily led to the murder, but Rachel herself blamed the shooting on the volatile relationship she had with her father.

The night before Thanksgiving, Rachel had been up late.

"My dad called me into his room and he asked me what I was still doing up. I told him I had been on the computer, and we started arguing. I remember, just at that point, it felt like nothing was ever going to get better, nothing was ever going to change, it was always going to be stress all the time," she said. "I knew things weren't going to get better once my mom passed. I knew I had bad years ahead of me."

She was sentenced to 18 years in prison for her mother's murder.

In 2016, two men were killed and seven people were injured on Thanksgiving in a shooting at Louisville's Shawnee Park.

The shooting started with an argument, and the first victim was a man who stepped between the two in order to prevent any violence, since there were children present at the park.

"Don't do this here, there are children," said 32-year-old William McKee, just before he was shot in an argument that wasn't his at all.

The shootings took place at the city's annual Juice Bowl family football competition, an event that had lured numerous community members including Louisville Mayor Greg Fischer, who was only 200 feet from the shooting.

The incident began when two men with a history of problems, Michael L. Carter and Michael Ricketts, saw each other and started shouting.

McKee knew both men, so he attempted to keep the peace.

Instead, after Ricketts punched Carter, according to witnesses, Carter pulled out a gun and shot, although the bullet meant for Ricketts instead hit McKee. A second bullet hit its intended target.

When Carter attempted to make a run for it, friends of both Ricketts and McGee pulled out their own weapons, and the area was peppered with gunfire.

Carter was shot several times and died in the grass at the park.

McKee also died, but Ricketts survived the shooting.

CONCLUSION

It would be easy, then, after reading about the savage acts of a few sick people, to feel a different kind of hate, one aimed at those who threaten our safety and make our world a less safe place in which to live.

But that is counter-productive, as it answers an action with something people whose hatred bubbles over into violence want. They hope to spark terror. They want to cause people to bar their doors and live in constant fear.

Micah Fletcher, who survived the Portland train attack, reminds us to remember the true victims of hate and attempt to walk around in their shoes for a while in order to understand how hard it is living in the shadow of such hatred.

"The little girl who had the misfortune to experience what happened on that MAX, her life is never going to be the same," said Fletcher. "Imagine that for a second, being the little girl on the MAX. This man is screaming at you, his face is a pile of knives, his body is a gun. Everything about him is cocked, loaded, and ready to kill you.

There's a history here with this, you can feel that this has happened before, the only thing that was different was the names and faces. And then a stranger, two strangers, three strangers, come to your aid, they try to help you and that pile of knives just throws itself at them, kills them."

As we inch closer to the close of another decade, perhaps the heroes of these stories, those who risked their lives or in some cases sacrificed them can bring some peace to our hearts.

MORE BOOKS BY JACK ROSEWOOD

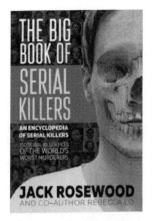

There is little more terrifying than those who hunt, stalk and snatch their prey under the cloak of darkness. These hunters search not for animals, but for the touch, taste, and empowerment of human flesh. They are cannibals, vampires and monsters, and they walk among us.

These serial killers are not mythical beasts with horns and shaggy hair. They are people living among society, going about their day to day activities until nightfall. They are the Dennis Rader's, the fathers, husbands, church going members of the community.

This A-Z encyclopedia of 150 serial killers is the ideal reference book. Included are the most famous true crime serial killers, like Jeffrey Dahmer, John Wayne Gacy, and Richard Ramirez, and not to mention the women who kill, such as Aileen Wuornos and Martha Rendell. There are also lesser known serial killers, covering many countries around the world, so the range is broad.

Each of the serial killer files includes information on when and how they killed the victims, the background of each killer, or the suspects in some cases such as the Zodiac killer, their trials and punishments. For some there are chilling quotes by the killers themselves. The Big Book of Serial Killers is an easy to follow collection of information on the world's most heinous murderers.

GET THESE BOOKS FOR FREE

Go to www.jackrosewood.com/free
and get these E-Books for free!

A NOTE FROM THE AUTHOR

Hello, this is Jack Rosewood. Thank you for reading this book. I hope you enjoyed the read. If you did, I'd appreciate if you would take a few moments to **post a review on Amazon.**

I would also love if you'd sign up to my newsletter to receive updates on new releases, promotions and a FREE copy of my Herbert Mullin E-Book, www.JackRosewood.com

Thanks again for reading this book, make sure to follow me on Facebook.

Best Regards
Jack Rosewood

11795455R00160

Made in the USA
Lexington, KY
15 October 2018